Sensitive Rhetorics

Pittsburgh Series in Composition, Literacy, and Culture

David Bartholomae and Jean Ferguson Carr, Editors

Sensitive Rhetorics

Academic Freedom and Campus Activism

Kendall Gerdes

University of Pittsburgh Press

Published by the University of Pittsburgh Press, Pittsburgh, Pa., 15260
Copyright © 2024, University of Pittsburgh Press
All rights reserved
Manufactured in the United States of America
Printed on acid-free paper
10 9 8 7 6 5 4 3 2 1

Cataloging-in-Publication data is available from the Library of Congress

ISBN 13: 978-0-8229-4811-7
ISBN 10: 0-8229-4811-7

Cover photo: Parbita Dutta
Cover design: Melissa Dias-Mandoly

For Kahlo, the joy of my heart
And for Erika, my condition of possibility

Contents

Acknowledgments

Sensitive Rhetorics was written in the midst of turmoil, instability, political distress, and pandemic. More times than I care to say over the life of this project, I felt deflated: all the air going out from my lungs, a slump hitting my shoulders. These feelings of disappointment and disillusionment weren't simply coincidental to this project. They also sensitized me, made me sensitive to claims about sensitivity. Writing is a gift, and it can also be difficult work. I want to acknowledge the difficulty so that I may more accurately honor all the sources of support and inspiration that kept me and this project afloat. Inspiration is a remedy when you're feeling deflated. Inspiration is literally the air rushing back into your lungs.

I first want to acknowledge the American Indian and Indigenous Peoples on whose lands this book was written: in Austin, Texas: the Alabama-Coushatta, Caddo, Carrizo/Comecrudo, Coahuiltecan, Comanche, Kickapoo, Lipan Apache, Tonkawa, and Ysleta Del Sur Pueblo; in Lubbock, Texas: the Comanche and Mescalero Apache; in Salt Lake City, Utah: the Shoshone, Paiute, Goshute, and Ute Tribes. Today, approximately 11.3 million American Indian, Alaska Native, and Native Hawaiian or other Pacific Islander peoples live in the United States. The ongoing legacies of violence, displacement, migration, and settlement in the United States continue to shape the universities I've learned and worked in.

I thank the supportive colleagues who joined me week after week in writing accountability groups, first the Women Faculty Writing Group at Texas Tech University and then the Scholarly Writing Collective at the University of Utah. Special thanks to Cassie Christopher for sharing this necessary advice at the right time: "My mantra for revising: If you're making it better, keep going; if you're just making it different, stop." Thanks to all those who read and offered me feedback on drafts and proposals, including my outstanding former colleagues at Texas Tech University: Michael Faris, Kristen Moore, Jennifer Nish, Lisa Phillips, Beau Pihlaja, Scott Wheedon, Greg Wilson, and Rachel Wolford. Thanks to my wonderful colleagues at the University of Utah and to my research assistant for 2022, Cody Page, whose position was funded by the university's Undergraduate Research Opportunities Program. Thanks to many other colleagues and comrades around the

United States and the globe: Ryan Skinnell, Andrea Alden, Judy Holiday, Neil Simpkins, Will Burdette, Rhiannon Goad, Beck Wise, Jennifer LeMesurier, and Timothy Oleksiak. For their mentorship and friendship, thanks to Josh Gunn and Diane Davis. And to Eric Detweiler and Steven LeMieux, thank you for always being willing to explore the unresolvable questions with me, from first premises down to prepositions.

I would also like to thank the graduate students I have taught and advised, including Nikki Borrenpohl, Casey Akins, Kimberly Fain, Marlene Galván, Leslie Hankey, Andrew Hollinger, Manny Piña, Janene Davison, Theresa Walsh, and Nkenna Onwuzuruoha. Students and scholars, your passion, your persistence, and your successes are energizing—and your willingness to be vulnerable as you work(ed) through the challenges of graduate school has been exemplary.

I have also been inspired by the persistence of so many theorists and scholars whose vital words helped make a home for me in the academy. The Rhetoric Society of America summer seminar Rhetoric and Sensation (2015) was a welcoming and formative site for my inquiry into sensitivity. I presented portions of this research to attentive and insightful audiences at the Rhetoric Society of America Conference, the Conference on College Composition and Communication, the Modern Language Association Conference, and the Center for Lesbian and Gay Studies Conference, as well as at the University and Micro-dynamics of Institutional Life Conference in Essex, where Jennifer Doyle's keynote demonstrated a discernment regarding our relation to academic institutions that was both instructive and humbling for me.

I thank the reviewers for their careful and perceptive feedback on this manuscript, as well as the publishing team at University of Pittsburgh Press who brought it to fruition. Thanks also to my developmental editor Lindsey M. P. Gay of Better Books Editing (and of SEIU 925!) for their early advice and reinforcement. And thank you to the senior scholars who wrote letters of recommendation, many times, when I sought grant funding to support this research. Of course, any errors are mine. I owe a debt of gratitude to so many others who contributed to making this publication possible.

My thanks also belong to student activists, especially you who are giving your all and getting back something you can't quite explain. You are exhausted but committed. Please don't burn yourselves out; remember to find what brings you joy. I hope this book affirms you and affirms that your work matters.

Thanks especially to the friends and writing companions who kept me accountable to the practice of writing: Laura K. Wallace, Sarah Murray, and Susan J. Loveall. And to the friends and loved ones who helped sustain me, especially in the lean years of pandemic, not least by looking after my child:

Lezlie Frye and Jacoby Ballard, Beth and Spencer Hardy, Aaron Gerdes and Abbey Gibb, and Kindra Nuñez. For their immeasurable contributions in that department and many others, thank you to my parents, Mary and Randy Gerdes.

Most of this writing took place in campus and home offices, but it also took place on a cell phone, in a rocking chair, and while a toddler napped on my shoulder, and I hope those passages will be the ones highlighted most often.

Thank you to my wife, Erika, who has unfailingly supported me in the pursuit of my academic goals. In sometimes untenable circumstances, you've always made me laugh. Our partnership is the root of who I am and who I want to grow to be. And thanks to my astounding child and joy machine, Kahlo: each day you inspire me anew. You keep the wind in my sail.

Finally, in memory of my canine companion and joy of a boy, Buckley Wheatsworth Gerñez, who shared his finitude with me and mine. Across our absolute dissymmetry, there you are in my heart.

Chapter 1 has been revised from a previously published article: Kendall Gerdes, "Trauma, Trigger Warnings, and the Rhetoric of Sensitivity," *Rhetoric Society Quarterly* 49, no. 1 (2019): 3–24, copyright the Society, available online: https://www.tandfonline.com/doi/full/10.1080/02773945.2018.1479767.

Chapter 4 has been revised from a previously published chapter: Kendall Gerdes, "Campus Carry, Academic Freedom, and Rhetorical Sensitivity," in *Rhetoric and Guns*, edited by Lydia Wilkes, Nate Kreuter, and Ryan Skinnell, 151–68 (Louisville, CO: University Press of Colorado/Utah State University Press, 2022).

Sensitive Rhetorics

Introduction

Being Sensitive and Rhetorical Being

> For there to be any sharing of symbolic meaning . . . a more originary
> rhetoricity must already be operating, a cons[t]itutive persuadability
> and responsivity that testifies, first of all, to a fundamental structure
> of exposure.
>
> **Diane Davis,** *Inessential Solidarity*

In a tweet first posted in late 2014, Sara Ahmed contends that sensitivity is not the deficit or liability that it's often made out to be, but an asset for subjects, and students specifically, in the struggle to survive: "Over-sensitive subjects / over-sensitive students are our best chance for survival." This book follows Ahmed's provocative claim and aims to theorize *sensitivity* as a rhetorical term of art, one that names the affective and even traumatic powers of language. In late 2014, there was a bloom of public controversy surrounding proposals that college instructors adopt the practice of using trigger warnings in their classes. While such proposals were actually quite few in number (two), the topic of trigger warnings became a site of passionate arguments about the powers of language and representation, as well as the responsibility of college and university teachers to their students.[1]

The debate about trigger warnings marked a new permutation in arguments about higher education in America. The critiques of political correctness that had permeated the 1990s (and that also tended to target campus culture) had lost much of their traction (Weigel 2016). By mid-2015, critiques of students who might request or benefit from trigger warnings were very frequently delivered as critiques of students' sensitivity (see Hanlon 2015; Vivian 2023). *Sensitive Rhetorics* examines debates over trigger warnings along with debates over several other contemporary student activist issues in which claims about sensitivity were mobilized as critiques of students. As I'll demonstrate, claims about sensitivity are also claims about rhetorical theory: about what language, teaching, and activism can and should do. I propose that a rhetorical theory of sensitivity can equip scholars and teachers to meet student activism with a more ethical response in our scholarship and pedagogy.

Unsurprisingly in controversies related to higher education, many debates over contemporary student activism feature powerful appeals to academic freedom. Casting academic freedom as threatened or besieged is likely to elicit strong reactions from members of the higher education community, for whom academic freedom is a dearly held value. But like many beloved values, academic freedom is also a complex topos, imbricated with the beliefs and ideological commitments that help define it (see Cole, Cole, and Weiss 2015). Academic freedom is a site of disagreement, but as a topos, it also functions as a site of invention, of the production and circulation of arguments (Eberly 2000, 5). While there is a small body of legal precedent that delineates academic freedom in the United States, many scholarly and even popular treatments of the topic have been published in recent years. Perhaps the most widely held view of academic freedom is one that conflates it with First Amendment rights to freedom of speech and expression, arguing that academic freedom ought to serve the marketplace of ideas in which unrestrained competition is imagined to give rise to the best or most true lines of thinking. This neoliberal view of academic freedom, which advantages the corporate interests of universities, has been especially effective at recruiting adherents from all over the ideological spectrum to share in an essentially conservative and often outright reactionary critique of students' sensitivity.

Sensitive Rhetorics asks why appeals to academic freedom are often able to turn professors, even those with otherwise progressive values, against students. Across several different campus issues, critics have argued that the "sensitivity" of student activists poses a threat to academic freedom. Such critiques of sensitive students have the effect of redirecting public argument away from the policy issues to which student activists were responding and shifting the ground of the argument to the values of free speech and academic freedom instead. By analyzing critiques of sensitivity as they have circulated in public arguments about a range of campus issues, *Sensitive Rhetorics* challenges the common sense of such critiques and argues for the theoretical importance of "sensitivity" to rhetoric. I demonstrate that critiques of sensitivity mark a deep (though not necessarily conscious) ideological discomfort with the idea that language is a form of action, from the ancient sophistic view of language as intoxicating to the postmodern view of language as instantiating. A more "sensitive rhetoric" would affirm the power of language to injure, wound, or harm, since, as I argue, this power is a condition for rhetorical existents—or we might say, social beings—to relate to and affect one another.

The main argument of this book is that critics of "sensitive students" are missing the way that sensitivity is a condition of possibility for the work of teaching and learning that's central to the purpose of higher education. Through rhetorical analysis of the "sensitivity" debates I have selected, I theorize sensitivity as the condition of possibility for language to both injure, wound, or harm, and to affect rhetorical existents in the first place. The claims about sensitivity that circulate in these debates are also claims about the nature and power of language as well as pedagogy. By studying these claims and how they circulate, how they attach to powerful values like academic freedom, we can better understand the beliefs, values, and material investments that shape these debates.

Sensitive Rhetorics intervenes in these ongoing debates by surfacing submerged assumptions about higher education, the role of instructors and faculty, and the needs of an increasingly diverse student body. These assumptions frequently appear as premises, stated or unstated, in contemporary arguments about campus issues. University and college campuses are a focal point for public debate about the power of language to injure or do harm in part because the pedagogical relationship is always a rhetorical relationship in which parties are vulnerable to being affected by one another in language. *Sensitive Rhetorics* challenges the construction of students and faculty as occupying opposing sides in these debates.

College campuses are also once again the focal point of a renewed culture war, which is to say: a contest over the definition and position of crucial public values, including freedom of speech and of inquiry, an informed and democratic citizenry, disciplinary knowledge, professional expertise, and the rigorous critique of cultural norms. *Sensitive Rhetorics* contends that rhetorical theory and analysis can make important contributions to ordinary public decision-making, especially where community values meet concerns about ethics, justice, and effective rhetorical action. Building a theoretical case grounded in the conjuncture of activism and academia, this book contributes to a growing literature on social justice in university life. As Sara Ahmed argues (2012), doing activist work in higher education can also teach us about the institutional rhetorics of universities and the complex interchange between social justice organizing and institutional policymaking.

Sensitive Rhetorics joins an ongoing conversation in rhetorical studies about ethics, hospitality, and responsibility. Drawing on recent and influential works in the field, I argue that rhetoric is fundamentally relational, and that rhetorical relationships create ethical obligations and responsibilities that may sometimes conflict and may not always be reconcilable. *Sensitive Rhetorics* builds on earlier explorations of hospitality and rhetoricity (e.g., Davis 2010; J. Brown 2015; Rollins 2020) by examining how "sensitivity" functions as a figure for beliefs about rhetorical power and relationality in public debates, and it further theorizes sensitivity as a constitutive condition for being affected by language in a rhetorical relation. Grounded in accounts of specific student activist interventions and debates, *Sensitive Rhetorics* makes a case for the utility of rhetorical theory in understanding and responding to urgent political issues, and specifically for understanding how public rhetorics shape both public policy and pedagogical practice.

The public and academic values at stake in sensitivity debates are also *rhetorical* values. At stake is whether knowledge is an object that can be mastered and transmitted or a contingent construct of language and culture. At stake is how to establish, recognize, and make use of expertise if knowledge is something *other* than simple and objective. At stake is whether academic freedom would best be understood itself as the object of disciplinary knowledge, or rather as a condition of disciplinarity and interdisciplinarity as such. At stake is the role of education in a democratic society, and the responsibility of teachers to their students and to the wider public. At stake is the relationship between the work of scholarship and justice, if rhetoric is indeed an art of justice, that is, of living together with people who are different from us. At stake is how we (should) conduct scholarly inquiry and instruction, and ultimately whether or not public trust will remain vested in universities as sites of knowledge-making.

Sensitivity: A Common Thread

While the body chapters of this book focus on some of the most prominent domains of debate about sensitivity and academic freedom in the last decade—policies pertaining to trigger warnings, Title IX, safe spaces, and campus carry—there are undoubtedly other examples one could choose, entangled in much the same milieu as that which I analyze in the chapters that follow. As academic freedom is repeatedly invoked to bolster arguments about political and practical decisions, it becomes bound up in different ideologies and rhetorical ecologies. A common thread runs through many stories from scenes of contest over higher education: they are narrated as a battle between factions. Students are made out to be overly sensitive and overly censorious, while reactionaries within as well as outside the academy attempt to occupy the ground of free inquiry and debate. This drama has had a powerful influence on media and popular understandings of higher education, evidenced in TV series such as Netflix's *Dear White People* (2017–2021) and, more recently, *The Chair* (2021). Students are construed as extremely powerful, and whatever light is shed on the influence of alumni and donors in directing the action of university administrations, even in response to crises—such as escalating outbreaks of racist violence on campus—it doesn't outshine the spotlight on the sensitivity of students.

Many of the contemporary controversies that student activists are surfacing and engaging in are instructive for scholars and observers, not only in and of themselves but as sites of public debate about community values. By looking at the arguments that circulate about sensitivity, we can examine (dominant) beliefs about how rhetorical agency and effectivity do or should function. Public rhetorics have policy implications, as well as pedagogical implications. Rhetorical theory can help us illuminate the implications of public critiques of sensitivity for public policy and for our classrooms.

My aim over the course of the chapters that follow is to build a theory of rhetorical sensitivity through analysis of contemporary student activist issues in which sensitivity has been at stake. In some cases, sensitivity is invoked overtly and often, whereas in others, similar arguments are encoded in terms of gender or race—or through the power fantasy attached to carrying a gun. Although it appears differently across these different areas of concern, *sensitivity* is the central term that delineates the scope of this project. Yet debates about sensitivity in higher education have been largely shaped by the circulation of arguments about academic freedom, specifically by worries that student activists will dismantle it. The relationship between these terms—*sensitivity* and *academic freedom*—illuminates the rhetorical landscape on which these debates play out. Although sensitivity is construed by its critics as the defining weakness of a generation (or two), I contend that sensitivity is a precondition for the process of inquiry and learning that academic freedom is meant to protect.

In the following section, I introduce relevant scholarship from three areas: academic freedom studies, rhetorics of student activism, and rhetorical theories of responsibility. Together these areas delimit the scope of this project, orbiting the central theme of sensitivity. This introduction contends that rhetorical theory is a crucial lens for making sense of the competing values attached to academic freedom, and of the ways they become articulated to and with pedagogy and policy in higher education. After all, debates over the proper relationships between knowledge, expertise, disciplinarity, education, democracy, and justice are debates that have defined the scope of rhetorical inquiry for millennia.

Conceptual Background: Academic Freedom

In a 2009 special issue of *South Atlantic Quarterly* dedicated to academic freedom, Jeffrey Nealon wrote that debates about academic freedom are largely confined to the university. But by the onset of the trigger warnings controversy just five years later, appeals to academic freedom had multiplied as issues in higher education garnered attention from a broader public. Often misunderstood as simply a special campus version of free speech, academic freedom is actually a legal doctrine, comprising a relatively small number of court decisions. But it's also a folk doctrine, by which I mean that both scholarly and nonexpert commentaries have contributed a lot to how academic freedom is defined and invoked in public arguments (Byrne 1989; Hofstadter and Metzger 1955; Menand 1996).

7

For the purposes of this book, it's important to see how faculty-centered appeals to academic freedom attach to and circulate alongside other (sometimes even competing) values and ideological commitments. Most often these include views about the proper production of disciplinary knowledge, the proper circulation of expertise through a credentialing and scholarly peer review, and the proper limitations of professionalism in a given discipline (Fish 2014). Propriety is key. Other arguments may invoke the value to the common good of a well-educated or well-informed democratic citizenry (Post 2012; Scott 2019), the highly esteemed freedoms of speech and expression, and the right and necessity of subjecting even widely accepted cultural and disciplinary norms to vigorous critique (Butler 2006). Yet one of the most fraught topoi connected to academic freedom in recent years is sensitivity.

Academic freedom bears a complex relationship to sensitivity. Most foregrounded in the past decade of debates about higher education is a relation of antagonism, in which sensitivity is construed as a, if not *the*, primary threat to academic freedom of our time. Sensitive students are said to be censorious students, able to effectively pressure faculty as well as administrators to remove topics, curricula, and even instructors from their classrooms if their sensitivities are offended. That there are, in fact, limits in both legal and folk doctrines to what academic freedom can protect, both inside and outside the classroom, does not seem to register a wrinkle of cognitive dissonance. Nor do the sensitivities of lobby groups, corporate donors, or alumni donors (McGee 2021) seem to be counted among the threats, which should tell us how the critics of sensitivity view money and status as determiners of whose sensitivity is truly threatening.

Sensitivity has also been said to be a key factor in self-censorship, often described in terms of a chilling effect. Under the floating sign of "viewpoint diversity,"[2] arguments about the value of conservative as well as regressive political viewpoints are mostly articulated as arguments about how students' sensitivity makes the people who hold those viewpoints feel unwelcome in the academy (without a trace of irony—see Handa 2019). Although these types of political opinions are comparatively underrepresented in higher education, the available data still shows they do outpace the presence of people from underrepresented groups, especially at higher ranks (even according to data presented by conservative scholars to support their self-description as an endangered minority in academia, see Shields and Dunn 2016, 2; cf. National Center for Education Statistics 2021a). Yet conservatives hold the megaphone, at least insofar as their complaints about representation are more commonly amplified in mainstream media (and in state legislatures) than those of other minority groups in higher ed. This disparity should tell us where in the academy the deposits of rhetorical power still lie.

Understanding what types of arguments academic freedom has been claimed to shield—and where it *has* failed—is key context for critiques of sensitivity. Academic freedom failed to shield Steven Salaita when his appointment at the University of Illinois was abruptly rescinded in 2014 after reactionary outcry over Salaita's tweets about the state of Israel's bombing of Palestine. Former chancellor Phyllis Wise bowed to pressure from donors, an action that in itself exposed the institution to liability. She resigned, and the university settled Salaita's lawsuit. But the damage to Salaita's career was already done (Cloud 2015). Academic freedom does not protect scholars, especially those engaged in public intellectual work, from coordinated harassment campaigns, like those weathered by Dana Cloud, Saida Grundy, and many others (Cloud 2017; Kamenetz 2018). Academic freedom does not even effectively prop up the tenure system when a governor or state board of regents aims to dismantle or defang it, as in Wisconsin in 2015 and in Georgia in 2021. Nor does academic freedom seem to influence labor conditions for contingent faculty, grad students, or even tenured and tenure-track professors, not even in the midst of the ongoing global COVID-19 pandemic (Zahneis 2018). In fact, the relative strength of appeals to academic freedom seems to grow when its force is exerted downward: by state legislatures against public universities, by university administrators against faculty, and by faculty against students. This does not paint a pretty portrait of the relation between academic freedom and rhetorical power: academic freedom is often an ineffective shield for those with less institutional status, and an effective cudgel for those who already have more power.

And yet, academic freedom is supposed to provide insulation for those with less rhetorical power to criticize even the most dominant norms and beliefs. Judith Butler contends: "As long as voices of dissent are only admissible if they conform to accepted professional norms, then dissent itself is limited so that it cannot take aim at those norms that are already accepted and, hence, cannot inaugurate new fields or disciplinary paradigms" (2006, 114). Stanley Fish (2014) has argued that critique is only proper in a discipline when it is delivered in terms and style acceptable to peer experts who have established and maintained the very norms under fire. (It's worth asking here how expertise is actually valued in higher education: as a classification of mastery over a body of knowledge, or as an academic commodity and metric for retention, tenure, and promotion. The neoliberal interests of universities may be served by commodifying faculty expertise, even in ways that part with the interests of faculty themselves.) Fish's resistance to critique has some alarming consequences: it leads him to attack faculty shared governance, implying that administrators have their own form of expertise when it comes to tuition, fees, staff, resources, and parking structures, so faculty ought best to stay out of their way and separate our work from their nonacademic decisions.

The problem with this view strict view of academic freedom as an accessory of professionalism is that resources such as tuition and fees (and yes, even parking structures) affect access, for students as well as for faculty and staff. And access is more than simply enrolling in (or being hired by) the university, since access can be throttled even while one attends class, completes a graduate degree, or works as a professor (Price 2021). As Butler (2013) argues in an essay on academic freedom in the context of the Israeli state occupation of Palestine: "Academic freedom can only be exercised when the material conditions for exercising those rights are secured, which means that infrastructural rights are part of academic freedom itself." Academic freedom is underpinned by its material conditions (see also Bérubé and Ruth 2015), and freedom of expression can be impinged upon not only by outright censorship but also by denying the possibility of its exercise—such as by denying freedom of movement (see also Butler 2015). If requests for access can be effectively pitted against academic freedom, however, then the people requesting are more easily dismissed as lazy, coddled, and overly sensitive.

In *Freedom of Speech and the Function of Rhetoric in the United States*, Michael Donnelly argues that free speech is a contingent and cultural value tied up with society's beliefs about the proper uses of rhetoric. Academic freedom is similarly implicated in cultural beliefs about rhetoric, teaching, and knowledge. The sophistic view that rhetoric is an art of justice, that goodness, wisdom, and virtue can be cultivated and taught, and that knowledge is a construct best measured by its utility to humankind yields a very different approach to academic freedom than the view that knowledge is a product of professional training in disciplinary inquiry and rhetoric, at best, a handy way to convey it. In the age of Facebook, YouTube, and TikTok algorithms, in which populist suspicion of scholarly expertise and credentialed scientific authority can be measured by flattened rates of COVID vaccinations coupled with exhortations to "do your own research," it is not guaranteed that the responsible exercise of scholarship—the performance of research and teaching—is going to remain vested in universities (see boyd 2018). If we want it to, we have to win a public argument about the goals and values of academic freedom (see Moody-Adams 2015; also Bérubé and Ruth 2022).

At stake are the reasons people choose to go to college, the financial investment of the state in assisting them, and in remunerating professors, instructors, graduate students, and other staff for their contributions to students' education and to a body of knowledge. In other words, at stake are people's lives and livelihoods, to say nothing of the quality of knowledge, deliberation, citizenship, democracy, and justice that the labor of scholarly work ultimately serves (or ought to serve). Should our lives and livelihoods depend on universities? Critiquing students for the neoliberal values of their universities does not seem like an adequate response to this question. In fact, doing so is a reactionary response that serves neoliberal ideology itself by settling blame on those actors with the least amount of agency in the institution.

Rhetorics of Student Activism

The fact that critiques of sensitivity have found a vein in which to circulate by targeting student activists necessitates an understanding of the rhetorical issues connected to student activism. What makes activism effective and sustainable? Recent social movement scholarship has emphasized the necessity of coalition building for successful activism, as in Karma Chávez's *Queer Migration Politics: Activist Rhetoric and Coalitional Possibilities* (2013). Erin Rand's *Reclaiming Queer: Activist and Academic Rhetorics of Resistance* (2014) also centers the importance of activist worldmaking practices in terms of both rhetorical invention and queer survival (see also Calafell and Ore 2021). Jennifer Nish's *Activist Literacies: Transnational Feminisms and Social Media Rhetorics* (2022) emphasizes the relational aspects of activism, examining the affordances of digital platforms for connecting activists with one another and across movements. Roderick A. Ferguson's *We Demand: The University and Student Protests* (2017) addresses student activists themselves, aiming to make usable some of the key insights from Ferguson's earlier book, *The Reorder of Things: The University and Its Pedagogies of Minority Difference* (2012). Student activism—especially that which is rooted in the liberation of Black, queer, feminist, and disabled people—is about making a more just and livable world. When student activists target their critiques and demands at their own institutions, it is also about making their campuses more hospitable places to learn.

Not all student activism is animated by a vision of justice and a more progressive future; critical exceptions to these claims would include student organizations such as the reactionary Turning Point USA (see Boedy 2022) or Young Americans for Freedom (Hatemi 2021), the anti-feminist women's group the Network of enlightened Women, and Students for Concealed Carry (on the latter's astroturf—i.e., fake grassroots—origins, see chapter 4). The existence of such groups demonstrates that a diversity of opinion does exist on college campuses, which is to say that higher education is simply not a successful left-wing indoctrination factory. At many campuses in recent years, local chapters of the College Republicans have wielded substantial power to attract media attention and provoke disruption by inviting high-profile conservative speakers such as Ann Coulter, Turning Point's Charlie Kirk, or the one-time Republican darling Milo Yiannopoulos (for more on Yiannopoulos's campus harassment tactics, see chapter 1). Events like this can draw considerable resources from public institutions, who are required to pay for security when protests and counterprotests crop up in anticipation or response. Such provocations are strategic for those who wish to characterize higher education as inhospitable both to conservatives and to the exercise of free speech. Rescinding, canceling, or even simply challenging the invitations to their platforms that right-wing student groups may extend makes colleges and universities appear to be censorious (for more on "deplatforming" and campus guest speakers, see the conclusion). Student activism is not just one thing; it does not pull institutions in just one direction.

Whether progressive activism in higher education is itself a viable project is a central question for the emerging field of critical university studies. Matthew Boedy's *May 1970* (2020) takes the month's twin occasions of law enforcement violence against student protestors (at Kent State University and at the historically Black college Jackson State University) as points of departure for examining long-standing tensions in composition studies between radical pedagogy and the field's disciplinary and professional status. Sara Ahmed's indispensable work on diversity, equity, and inclusion rhetoric demonstrates the way institutions can co-opt even radical critiques (albeit not without tension, or we might say indigestion). *On Being Included: Racism and Diversity in Institutional Life* (2012) examines, through interviews with what Ahmed terms "diversity practitioners," how transformative work in universities has been limited by, resisted by, and absorbed into existing university cultures and procedures. This dynamic is one of the steepest challenges student activists face (the other being the power of administrators to drag out responding to student activists and simply wait for them to graduate). Ahmed continues her examination of what she terms "institutional mechanics" (6) in *Complaint!* (2021), tracing how the circulation and consequences of complaints (or the lack thereof) can teach us about how an institution works. *Sensitive Rhetorics* offers a way to conceptualize the strategic vulnerabilities of colleges and universities through the institutional rhetoric of sensitivity.

Institutional rhetoric offers an important perspective on student activism. Ryan Skinnell, in "Toward a Working Theory of Institutional Rhetorics," reminds us of the many functions of institutions: they "foster—and sometimes betray—trust and dependency," "invent and ossify customs," "discipline and normalize institutional actors," and "serve as arbiters of symbolic value," to mention a few (2019, 78). Institutional rhetoric examines the constellation of these functions and the incoherence or contradiction they can occasion. In their "Institutional Critique: A Rhetorical Methodology for Change," James E. Porter, Patricia Sullivan, Stuart Blythe, and others (2000) argue that institutions *are* changeable. They advocate for institutional critique as an activist methodology—that is, as a way of doing scholarship that also intervenes in institutional problems (see, e.g., Elder and Davila 2019). But they also point out that institutions can resist even ideologically successful arguments if material conditions could inhibit change. Thinking about the work of student activists as institutional critique can help us remember that students are scholars, too, and that sensitivity is not the sole province of students, since institutions also have their sensitivities. Louis M. Maraj, in his book *Black or Right: Anti/ Racist Campus Rhetorics* (2020), reminds us that institutions can act defensively, "preempt[ing] or skirt[ing] racial stress or even the subject of race to protect white feelings" (152n22). Defensiveness can be a sign of underlying vulnerability.

The rationale for academic freedom that links education to the common good is also relevant in thinking about rhetorics of student activism. Commonplaces about the link between education and democracy resonate throughout many histories of rhetoric as well as contemporary studies of democratic dialogue and deliberation (Asen 2015; Ben-Porath 2017; Boler 2006). As Rosa A. Eberly argues in *Towers of Rhetoric* (2018), many other cultural institutions, like TV or radio (or social media sites, for that matter), are "too interested in entertainment and ratings and profit margins to provide a place for publics to form by patiently allowing individuals to discover and discourse together about issues of common concern" (Archive 06). Eberly draws this conclusion: "The future of our democracy depends on public education" (Archive 06). Although our faith in this claim might be shaken by the ever-increasing interest of universities in entertainment and ratings and profit margins, I suspect that much of the rhetorical power of mobilizing academic freedom as a value derives from a continuing (if occasionally lapsed, or unrenewed) subscription to Eberly's claim. And it's not just what educators are doing that matters. It's what students can do when they have the chance, which colleges and universities can provide them with, to deliberate and act together on matters of public concern.

Yet, the chance to act together is not always yielded easily to students. Jonathan Alexander, Susan Jarratt, and Nancy Welch argue in their introduction to *Unruly Rhetorics: Protest, Persuasion, and Publics* (2018) that when a discourse resists the voices of outsiders, disruption and unruliness may be one way for those outsiders to find entry. Civility, with all that it implies about politeness and deference to authority, is a powerful constraint on student activism. In *Writing Against Racial Injury: The Politics of Asian American Student Rhetoric* (2015), Haivan V. Hoang shows how an Asian American student group suffered from placing too much trust in civility. Their institution's student government, failing to recognize the value of a diverse campus for all students, pulled financial support for an Asian American student mentorship program. In attempting to follow the prescribed institutional procedures, the activists sustained a significant and material loss. While Alexander, Jarratt, and Welch don't necessarily valorize unruliness in itself, drawing distinctions about the ethical purposes of disruption, they do underscore disruption's rhetorical force. And they remind us that an ethical rhetorical culture is not necessarily a civil or decorous one.

Rhetorical Theories of Responsibility

The question of what does make an ethical rhetorical culture brings me to the final area of conceptual background for this project: rhetorical theory, and specifically theories oriented toward exploring and cultivating responsible rhetoric. Judith Butler writes in *Excitable Speech: A Politics of the Performative*, "Does understanding from where speech derives its power to wound alter our conception of what it might mean to counter that wounding power?" (1997, 50). *Sensitive Rhetorics* attempts to respond to Butler's query, taking seriously not only the power of language to wound but the vulnerability of rhetorical existents to being wounded. Language injures, argues Butler, when and because it exposes the body of the addressee *as* vulnerable to address. This rhetorical exposedness is termed *rhetoricity* by Diane Davis, which she defines as "an affect*ability* or persuad*ability*," but which is actually not an *ability* at all (2010, 2). It is an incapacity, a *nonpower*: a sensitivity.

Sensitivity as a rhetorical term of art highlights the radical passivity of rhetorical existents—that is, our uncloseable openness to the address or affection of others. This openness is the condition of possibility for becoming a rhetorical subject. Although the rhetorical "agent" is not a sovereign, responsibility for the exercise of rhetorical power derives from this open space, from the ability to respond, and from the prior inability to stop oneself from being affected by an other. This undergoing of affection, this suffering or even passion, has been described by Jacques Derrida as a "nonpower at the heart of power" (2006, 28). *Sensitive Rhetorics* aims to inscribe these valences of rhetoricity, its traumatic force and even violence (see also Rollins 2009), but also the possibility it thereby generates for becoming otherwise.

These claims about the nature of rhetoric and reality may appear to be unqualified. In *The Ethical Fantasy of Rhetorical Theory* (2018), Ira J. Allen contends that the idea of foundational truth is a fantasy, but a necessary or at least inescapable one, and that the advantage of fantasy for rhetoric is in its radical contingency and thus alterability. We judge our theories of rhetoric by how well argued they are, and by how much they seem to describe or explain our objects (or, subjects) of study. The theory of rhetorical sensitivity articulated in this project is not proposed as a noncontingent foundation but rather as a new or next alteration in thinking about responsible rhetoric. Theory is not simply a tool for understanding; that instrumentalist view would recuperate it to the teleologies of clarity and knowledge. Rather, theory is a way of inventing those new and next alterations in thinking that are necessary for seeing things differently, and for changing the conditions that constrain what is possible (see Alden et al. 2019, 4).

If sensitivity names a vulnerability to rhetorical affection that both exceeds and underwrites the capacity of rhetorical existents to receive and respond to this affection, then sensitive rhetorics are those that take responsibility for the force of affection. This force may be effective or transformative, and it may also be violent, even traumatic—and sometimes all of these at once. Denying this will not make rhetoric more ethical. But to take up the work of sensitive rhetorics would mean doing scholarship in the pursuit of a more just and livable future.

Sensitivity, Vulnerability, and Wounding

Although I think *sensitivity* best names the irreparable rhetorical exposedness this book seeks to explore, I want to acknowledge the close connection to *vulnerability*, one I draw on throughout this book.[3] Philosopher Olúfẹ́mi O. Táíwò has asked "why 'I should be able to wound you' ended up the guiding frame for (some) discussions about sharing and intimacy?" (Táíwò 2021). In this light, calling for vulnerability could be understood as a call to submit or yield oneself to the power of others, even in its potential for harm or violence. Yet, as I contend, to be invulnerable would mean to be insensate, incapable of being affected. Being able to be wounded is an inextricable aspect of being able to be affected. In this book, I am by no means calling for a right to wound others, but for the development of a theory of rhetorical sensitivity that accounts for this power, and further takes responsibility for it. In *Precarious Life: The Powers of Mourning and Violence* ([2004] 2006), Judith Butler links the acknowledgment of others' vulnerability to the social granting of recognition that others' lives are grievable, that they count as human. Drawing on the work of philosopher Emmanuel Levinas, Butler identifies "a constant tension between the fear of undergoing violence and the fear of inflicting violence," a tension that stems from our mutual (if unevenly distributed) precarity (137). Butler argues that responding to another's address, and to the precarity that address communicates, is precisely what arouses this tension. One is sensitive to the other's address, without or against one's own will: "There is a certain violence already in being addressed, given a name, subject to a set of impositions, compelled to respond to an exacting alterity" (139). This violence of address is constitutive; we would never feel it, never be moved by the tension it excites, unless we first sense it—and the vulnerability it entails.

Methods and Research Artifacts

Methodologically, *Sensitive Rhetorics* necessarily draws from a variety of humanities fields, including feminist and queer theory, critical race theory, disability studies, affect theory, and continental philosophy. A range of disciplinary lenses are needed to apprehend the key issues raised by contemporary student activism, and since academic freedom itself subtends the establishment of criteria and norms for expertise in all disciplines. This book depends on rhetoric's capacity to incorporate multidisciplinary inquiry, a capacity that makes rhetoric a crucial field for scholarship that tests or exceeds the scope of traditionally siloed disciplinary works. My approach to rhetorical analysis is also inflected by Sharon Crowley (2006), who argues that rhetoricians should examine what beliefs and values are connected to an argument as it is circulated and changed by various parties to a public debate. Arguments are often taken up outside of the communities that originated them because of their appeal to some shared value, such as academic freedom—but such arguments may entail other submerged ideological commitments that rhetorical analysis can expose, explain, and ultimately intervene in.

Campus activism, and the public debates that swirl around it, can help illuminate the rhetorical, theoretical, and political issues at stake in these bodies of research. The research materials that delimit the debates under study in this project include public writing about these issues by students, scholars, administrators, and other commentators. I am interested in critiques of sensitivity that have been authored or amplified by members of the faculty, but I am also interested in instances of these critiques by outsiders, which evidence the influence and wide circulation of such arguments. Notably, though faculty members frequently tie their critiques of sensitivity to concerns about academic freedom, these critiques are often circulated, even by scholars, *outside* the context of scholarly peer review (e.g., in blog posts, or books published by popular presses). I am also interested in the way university and governmental policies stage or spotlight critiques of sensitivity, and the ways media coverage of student activism has circulated the same. Ultimately, all of these objects must be contextualized as satellites in the solar system of higher education, always moving in relation to the gravity of the university as an institution.[4]

Campus activism therefore anchors this study as the site of public debate about sensitivity. Although it's certainly not the only such site, debates about campus activism have preceded (or I might say portended) debates about sensitivity in other aspects of public life. Premises that first circulated in 2014 about the sensitivity of college students widened their scope in the years that followed to target whole constituencies of the US American public. Complaints about college students aren't a new phenomenon, but their rhetorical form reflects public beliefs about learning, higher education, and the purposes of universities. The critique of students' sensitivity circulated widely (and among disparate groups of stakeholders in higher education) in part because of its attachment to claims about the purpose and status of academic freedom. Academic freedom is a convenient proxy, rhetorically; outside the academy, sensitivity is said to infringe on the broader right of free speech instead. Academic freedom is a relevant and necessary topic for any analysis of contemporary debates about sensitivity in higher education; in each of the controversies detailed in the chapters that follow, claims about sensitivity and academic freedom can be found together, each shaping the form of the other. Students' sensitivity wouldn't be understood as a matter of public concern if it couldn't be construed as threatening a public value. In the context of higher education, academic freedom is this value. Beliefs about it therefore constrain as well as enable beliefs about sensitivity, helping them to circulate and find currency.

If one views academic freedom as ensuring an unregulated "marketplace of ideas," then any attempt to criticize or alter the rules of the "marketplace" will be viewed as unwarranted and overly sensitive. Invoking academic freedom alongside sensitivity effectively redirects public argument, shifting the grounds of debate away from activists' issues and toward what are essentially rhetorical values: the social role of debate itself, and the purposes of hearing, discussing, and responding to different ideas (and practices) than one's own. Theorizing sensitivity is necessary to demonstrate how a rhetorical relation underwrites both difference and debate, and this relation depends on the ability of rhetoric to move as well as to wound. No doctrine of academic freedom that discounts this rhetorical sensitivity is adequate to the pedagogical or ethical demands of our current moment.

After 2020?

What has become of the "grave threats" to academic freedom that have been named from across the political spectrum over the past several years? Can we say definitively yet whether trigger warnings and safe spaces have destroyed the US American academy? Can we say that Title IX and campus carry policies have made college campuses less safe and more hostile? Higher education has faced significant changes and challenges in recent years, and in the wake of 2020, which saw both the start of the COVID-19 pandemic in the United States and the loss of President Trump's bid for reelection. Can we say whether any of the threats to academic freedom supposedly posed by sensitivity that predated these events have subsided?

In Henry Reichman's *The Future of Academic Freedom* (2019), he argues that academic freedom has always been embattled. Pressure on and even threats to academic freedom come from dwindling state funding for higher education, replaced in university budgets with more tuition dollars and an increased reliance on the goodwill of private donors; from the erosion of shared governance, tenure, and labor protections as well as the ongoing adjunctification of the teaching faculty; and from plainly censorious state legislative battles, lately over racial sensitivity trainings that mention "white privilege" and all that's made to be represented under the sign of "critical race theory." Reichman also notes that "the physical safety of scholars—both students and faculty"—is increasingly jeopardized by harassment and threats of violence (2015, 249; see also Cloud 2017). The uptick in openly racist violence after President Trump's

2016 election only represented an intensification of hostility toward scholars of color that has shaped the US American academy since its inception.

So although the context for some of the issues analyzed in this book has changed over the years since the incidents I explore, we must remember that the context will keep on changing, and/but that there is no guarantee that these changes will always or overall represent progress. In fact, many of the debates examined here articulate backlash against progressive student activism that has never seemed to become self-aware of its consonance with regressive, reactionary politics. Even for those debates that many no longer feel of the present moment, we must pay attention to the way that arguments against sensitivity have developed, attaching themselves to values that help their circulation into wider public discourses and waiting for another moment of resurgence.[5] Readers who rode out the Trump years must not forget that the discursive conditions for the critiques of sensitivity analyzed here, and for Trumpism's political success, ripened in the Obama years. While Trump's executive orders about higher education have been rescinded, lasting damage has been done in federal Title IX policy, in moving the Overton window of state legislative priorities for both higher education and K–12, and in the ongoing contest over immigration policy and the legal status of DREAMers, and so on. "After" doesn't simply mean "over."

Moreover, the advent in 2020 of a global coronavirus pandemic has thrown higher education into turmoil that's long outlasted the initial response of emergency remote teaching. In the absence of federal policies, colleges and universities in the United States have found themselves at the mercy of state legislatures' attitudes toward COVID-19 vaccine requirements (the irony of long-standing MMR vaccine requirements notwithstanding) and mask-wearing. Yet many of the pre-pandemic concerns about mental health, sexual violence, racism, and other ordinary traumas that affect students' lives and abilities to learn have only intensified, refracted through periods of long isolation and low social support, and pocked with grief for imagined futures, lost loved ones, and an incomprehensible global and national death toll. Perhaps "after" COVID, the temptation will be stronger than ever to harden, to become insensitive and invulnerable against the affection of others, perceived as a potential threat. But I hope this book will remind its readers that disavowing sensitivity does not protect us, nor does it give us the space to grieve and to heal; if we let it, our sensitivity can open us to a more equitable and just landscape for higher education.

Outline of Chapters

The first chapter, "Sensitive Students: Trauma, Trigger Warnings, and Access," focuses on critiques of sensitivity in the debate over using trigger warnings in college classes. Students who advocate for using trigger warnings argue that language has the power to destabilize student survivors of trauma, and that trigger warnings are one way for instructors to help minimize the potential disruption caused by being triggered in a college class. Critics disavowed the rhetorical sensitivity of students and argued that academic freedom protected the right of instructors not only to select and assign course materials but also to challenge and even shock students for pedagogical reasons. Laying out the case for a rhetorical theory of trauma, chapter 1 contends that all rhetorical existents are vulnerable to one another because we are exposed to each other's affection in language. This chapter demonstrates the intervention that sensitive rhetorics can make in practical policy debates by surfacing the rhetorical consequences of how the trigger warnings debate has been argued. Beginning with this widely known campus issue, the first chapter illustrates the methods and theoretical framework that inform subsequent chapters. Sensitivity is not an ability; it is a condition of possibility for rhetorical affection and response that makes teaching and learning possible.

Chapter 2, "Sensitive Subjects: Sexual Misconduct Policy and Sexual Power," analyzes the trope of sensitivity in debates over campus sexual issues and Title IX. Student activists and advocates for Title IX see themselves as offering a critique of the operation of sexual power in institutions (see Ahmed 2017). Critics of Title IX argue that university Title IX proceedings violate the due process rights of the accused and encourage students to understand their sexuality as legally fraught and themselves as fragile victims—yet some critics, like Laura Kipnis, have come to see themselves as the real victims of Title IX and their opposition to the policy as a defense of academic freedom. I argue that critiques of sensitivity misrepresent or misunderstand student activists' arguments that sexual harassment is a form of institutional power. Following Jennifer Doyle's (2015) analysis of Title IX as "the administrative structure through which the university knows what exposure feels like" (24), I argue that an institutional rhetoric of sensitivity can help us understand the legal, financial, and ethical relations of the university as themselves structured by exposedness. Chapter 2 argues that while power can function to insulate sensitivity, even institutions are sensitive: an institutional rhetoric of sensitivity can help us understand the legal, financial, and ethical relations of the university as themselves structured by exposure.

The third chapter, "Racial (In)Sensitivity: Black Student Activism and the Demand for Safe Spaces," examines the wave of Black student-led occupations in 2015–2016, following the encampment of protestors on the University of Missouri's Carnahan Quad. Fora organized on campuses and online using the hashtag #BlackOnCampus articulated the commonality of negative experiences among Black students. Petitions like those published at TheDemands. org identified specific policy changes and other requests designed to improve and implement universities' efforts toward diversity and inclusion, and to make the on-campus life of students of color more equitable and more bearable. Yet critics complained that the efforts of Black students to establish safe spaces to discuss and organize in response to their experiences were exclusionary, overly sensitive, and undermined free and academic debate. I contend that the occupation illustrates José Esteban Muñoz's (2009) framework of utopian performativity—that is, it both names *and* instantiates a safer future for Black students by and through the rhetoric of the demand. Chapter 3 contends that sensitivity enables marginalized communities to engage in the very debates that their critics were calling for. Sensitivity itself can be utopian; it can be a way of instantiating a future even in the midst of an intolerable present.

Chapter 4 looks at a slightly different constellation of academic freedom and sensitivity on the issue of campus carry policies, which mandate that public universities and colleges must allow concealed handguns in their classrooms. In this case, faculty as well as students who oppose guns on campus *on the grounds of academic freedom* are the ones targeted by accusations of sensitivity. "Vulnerability to Violence: An Account of Campus Carry in Texas" draws on the history of campus carry policy in Texas as well as the unsuccessful lawsuit brought by professors at the University of Texas at Austin against state and university authorities on the grounds that Texas's campus carry law infringes on their constitutional rights. This chapter argues that the threat of violence places serious constraints on academic freedom, but that the campus carry debate shows that the value of academic freedom can be cut loose by critics on an issue where sensitivity and academic freedom appear to be aligned rather than opposed. Academic freedom and sensitivity are not incompatible values. Remaining sensitive means refusing to be indifferent to violence.

The conclusion condenses the argument of the book that sensitivity marks a place in public argument where our vulnerability to one another as rhetorical existents gets denied and even buried. This final chapter also draws out the implications that those of us committed to the value of academic freedom and to its place in the education of a democratic citizenry should not be persuaded by critiques of sensitivity but instead make sensitivity the basis of a more ethical rhetorical theory. Sensitive rhetorics can reshape these debates about university policy and culture.

Chapter 1

Sensitive Students

Trauma, Trigger Warnings, and Access

Over-sensitive can be translated as: sensitive to that which is not over.

Sara Ahmed, "Against Students"

At the tail end of 2013, *Slate* published an article declaring 2013 "The Year of the Trigger Warning" (Marcotte 2013). But if you'd paid hardly any attention at all to public controversies surrounding higher education in the ten years or so since then, you'd know it was in the years that followed that trigger warnings came into vogue as a topic of opinion journalism in such venues as the *New York Times*, the *LA Times*, the *Guardian*, *Mother Jones*, the *New Republic*, and *Salon*, as well as at the *Chronicle of Higher Education* and *Inside Higher Ed*. In fact, only halfway through 2014, more than fifty articles taking a stand against trigger warnings had been published (Yergeau 2014)—and they kept on coming. Most of these jeremiads blasted students for being too sensitive. Some critics characterized students who advocated for using trigger warnings in college classes as weak and vulnerable, ill-equipped to negotiate an academic environment. At the same time, they also characterized these sensitive students as powerful and influential, pressuring their institutions to tiptoe around students' feelings. Most of these op-eds were not penned by college teachers, though a few significant contributions were. This chapter examines the common premises that circulated in public arguments against using trigger warnings in college classes. I argue that such arguments amplified (and continue to amplify) a critique of sensitivity, which in turn is used to undermine the values of academic freedom that critics profess to hold.

Scholars and teachers of the humanities are especially targeted by critiques of the sensitivity of our students. There are two somewhat paradoxical reasons for this: first, because our curricula often raise what could be described as "sensitive" issues—gender, race, class, and the violence made or made possible by these ideological forces—and second, because we're imagined in the wider public as a bunch of "tenured radicals" (whether we're tenured or not—and, whether we're *radical* or not). When nonacademics claim that our students are coddled, fragile, and insulated from disagreement, they don't seem to imagine accounting or engineering professors are at fault. I don't at all mean that these fields are free from ideological controversies—only that when state legislators pore through college course listings for something to grandstand about, they start with the humanities (Herzog 2016). Yet scholars and teachers of rhetoric ought to be authorities on the questions that trigger warnings raise about the power and effectivity of language to pierce, wound, and open human beings to one another. As a rhetorician, I understand attacks on sensitivity to be embedded in multiple ideological contexts—that is, to be connected to other argumentative premises and beliefs that may be submerged or suppressed by the authors of such attacks, knowingly or not. This chapter uses the debate over trigger warnings as an occasion to investigate the repudiation of sensitivity and its rhetorical consequences.

This chapter opens *Sensitive Rhetorics* because the arguments against sensitivity that were incubated in the trigger warnings debate have since been deployed in a number of other campus issues, against higher education as a cultural institution and against the most vulnerable segments of academic communities. Most parties to the debate over trigger warnings seem to agree that the value of academic freedom, including how it gets defined and practiced at colleges and universities in the United States, is contested. To be sure, the political stakes are high. But there are also theoretical issues involved in denigrating the sensitivity of our students. The belief that *words matter* is a contested belief, perhaps more clearly now than at any previous time in US American history. I aim to show that "sensitivity" marks a fundamentally rhetorical exposedness, a vulnerability to being affected in language that impairs the self-containment of the rhetorical subject. While critics of trigger warnings accuse students of misunderstanding and even overstating their own experiences of harm and trauma, I hold that the sensitivity of students (as well as teachers) is what actually makes teaching and learning possible. If, following Kenneth Burke (1950), we define rhetoric broadly as "addressed" language (38), then sensitivity can be understood as a condition of possibility for one to be affected by an/other's address. As I'll show, without the route of affection that sensitivity opens up, the rhetorical subject would have no way of receiving, and no cause for responding to, anything outside itself.[1]

I understand the use of trigger warnings as an accessibility practice developed by and for survivors of trauma. "Trauma," of course, has several usages, including common, clinical, and psychoanalytic (Caruth 1996; Friedman 2012; Herman 1992; and see Hesford 1999, 195), but I also employ and develop it throughout this book as a theoretical term of art. But before wading into the theoretical claims of this chapter, I begin by reviewing the precipitating incidents in 2013–2014 when students made requests for trigger warnings at their schools. I then lay out the rhetorical commonplaces circulated against trigger warnings and against sensitive students. I argue that students' claim that trigger warnings are one way to make college classes more accessible was effectively sidelined by appeals to academic freedom. Such appeals, including defenses of even injurious speech, are at risk of co-optation into the service of reactionary political goals. I turn to the theory of hospitality to argue that accessibility and (more broadly) inclusion present us with ethical tensions that can't be easily resolved by recourse to academic freedom. Finally, I contend that a rhetorical theory of sensitivity can help members of the academy recognize that teaching and learning always take place in scenes of trauma, and that as teachers we are ethically implicated by the irreparable exposure to one another in language that "sensitivity" names. The aim of this book is to move the field toward a more sensitive rhetoric, toward rhetorics that acknowledge and respond to the power of language to injure, wound, or harm, and that accepts this power as constitutive of rhetorical existents.

Commonplaces in the Trigger Warnings Debate

A trigger warning is a designation that alerts a reader to something in the text they are about to read (or other media they are about to experience) that could be destabilizing. Such designations are often accompanied by an indicator of specific issues, such as "suicide" or "sexual violence." Readers who might be sensitive to mentions, discussions, or graphic descriptions of those issues are made aware of their presence in the text in advance of reading so that they will not be caught off guard. I draw this definition from rhetoricians and disability studies scholars, and I prefer it because it emphasizes the ability of words or representations to affect us without specifying a necessary outcome of this affection (Carter 2015; Livingston 2014; Orem and Simpkins 2015; Yergeau 2014). Being "triggered," as I'll explain later on, names a serious disruption to one's emotional, cognitive, and physical capacities.

During the academic year 2013–2014, two proposals to adopt the use of trigger warnings in college classes were introduced, and they quickly became flash points for a public debate over the norms and values of higher education. The first proposal came from the staff of Oberlin College and Conservatory's Office of Equity Concerns, which suggested that trigger warnings could be an effective accommodation for students dealing with trauma related to sexual assault ("Support" 2013). While students are most often depicted as the advocates of trigger warnings, the recommendation at Oberlin was developed by a task force that included a vice president and dean of students, three deans, a faculty member who became a dean after her appointment to the task force, two alumni, and three students (Flaherty 2014). The second proposal came in the form of a student senate resolution at the University of California, Santa

Barbara, and aimed to require instructors to list trigger warnings for course content on their syllabi. Of course, such a resolution would have to be adopted by an institutional body with binding authority over the faculty in order to *require* instructors to use trigger warnings, since a student government resolution alone has no such power.

So much ink was spilled (or digitally disseminated) over these two incidents that something of a misperception took hold not only among the general public but also among college and university faculty members. The vehemence of the opposition to using trigger warnings in college classes (with a few other rhetorical strategies to boot) made it seem that students had been overwhelmingly successful in making demands that would impinge on the freedom of faculty. But using trigger warnings had not actually become institutional policy (even at Oberlin or UCSB). In 2015, the National Coalition Against Censorship conducted an informal survey of Modern Language Association and College Art Association members; 808 respondents were asked whether their institutions had adopted a trigger warnings policy. Half a percent said yes, though it is likely that those four respondents were mistaken (Kingkade 2015). The report on the survey concluded that there is "no crisis, but deep concern," about trigger warnings (National Coalition Against Censorship 2015).

This "concern" was evident in the slew of opinion pieces that appeared starting in the spring of 2014 attacking students for being too sensitive. With few variations, critics of trigger warnings circulated a set of claims that rhetoricians might refer to as commonplaces—arguments (or premises in an argument) that reflect the common sense of a community. Versions of these claims can be found in a wide range of writing against trigger warnings (7 Humanities Professors 2014; Drum 2014; Duggan 2014; Filipovic 2014; Frank 2014; Halberstam 2014; J. Goldberg 2014; Kipnis 2015a; Lukianoff and Haidt 2015; Medina 2014; Milks 2014; and Wilson 2015, to name a few; for a review of the scientific research related to these claims, see Laguardia, Michalsen, and Rider-Milkovich 2017). One prominent commonplace about trigger warnings was the description of their "spread" to college campuses from their use on online forums and blogs (especially feminist blogs) as a virus or cancer. A related move was to place blame for the outbreak on coddled, entitled millennials, or teenagers, particularly users of the social media site Tumblr—Tumblr's reputation as the home of "social justice warriors" encodes critics' suspicion that digital activists aren't doing "real" or meaningful activism. Critics claimed that young people are more committed to the performance of outrage and a purist "callout culture" than to coalitional politics. Advocates of trigger warnings were said to be trying to hide from the real world, inflating their experiences of personal harm into trauma and spreading their own sensitivities onto others. Critics imagined an ever-expanding list of potential triggers, the presence of which would be forbidden, arguing that triggers could be anything—even smells. Some said only "exposure therapy" would help trauma survivors learn to face their triggers. They fretted, on the one hand, that students who did not have a disability legitimated by the student services office of their schools would start to use trauma as an excuse not to do their coursework, and on the other hand, that survivors of trauma should not reify the individualized medical model imposed by the student services offices. Critics suggested, some of them politely, that sensitive students should develop a sense of humor, grow a thicker skin, and learn to take a joke in order to deal with things they find hurtful or offensive. Asking instructors to make changes to the norms by which class is conducted, critics said, reflects the attitude not of a student but of a neoliberal consumer of education. Even the act of asking for trigger warnings was said to have a chilling effect on academic freedom and free speech. Instructors should make decisions about their teaching, critics held, without being subjected to students' demands. One particularly generic iteration of these commonplaces spread so widely and rapidly that even the American Association of University Professors directly copied a paragraph into their statement on trigger warnings, for which they later added a citation (Committee A 2014; Jarvie 2014).

One piece published in the *Chronicle of Higher Education* claimed (as late as 2015) that trigger warnings were evidence that "the gravest threat" facing the university today is the sensitivity of students (Bass and Clark 2015). Such apocalypticism makes sensitive students out to be worse for the future of academic freedom than corporate control of higher education; than campaigning by reactionaries to fire faculty for political remarks on social media, let alone remarks in their areas of expertise; than the erosion of tenure and faculty governance and rising reliance on contingent labor (see Bérubé and Ruth 2015); than even the literal presence of loaded guns in classrooms, as campus carry laws are adopted by more and more states. Neoliberal threats to the institution of higher education are plentiful, even if they are hard to measure precisely.

When opinions like those I have identified earlier find acceptance among many members of a community and circulate widely, rhetoricians call them *doxa*, or "commonplaces" (Crowley 2006, 47, 70–75). These commonplaces, many of which were put into circulation by opinion journalists, took hold among scholars and teachers of higher education in part because they served the purpose of confirming communally held values about academic freedom. Allegiance to the values that commonplaces activate can be so strong that appeals to those values override one's countervailing interests. For example, many of the same claims advanced by conservative critics of higher education (J. Goldberg 2014; Lukianoff and Haidt 2015) also appeared in the public and scholarly writing of queer and feminist scholars (7 Humanities Professor

2014; Duggan 2014; Halberstam 2014; Halberstam 2017). I suspect that it was the resonance of the appeal to academic freedom that underpinned this alliance of opinion.

Academic freedom is a partly legal and partly folk doctrine that some argue should extend to cover not only research but also what college teachers may teach and how they may teach it. For scholars, academic freedom is a highly resonant community value, even though it's legally far less robust than often imagined. Case law in the United State has most frequently protected the autonomy of the institution, and sometimes expressly not the autonomy of the faculty (Gajda 2009, 104). In 2009, Jeffrey Nealon wrote that discussion of academic freedom has "largely been confined to the university" (753), but the trigger warnings debate seems to mark a significant inflection point for discussions of academic freedom reaching (and involving) a wider public. Of course, it's teachers and scholars whose employment is bound up with academic freedom in law and policy. In an article published on *Inside Higher Ed* in 2014, a group of authors calling themselves "7 Humanities Professors" argued that untenured and contingent faculty, and scholars whose writing and teaching is critical of hegemonic norms, could be exposed to increased complaints about their teaching made by students to administrators, which could put their academic freedom—and their jobs—in jeopardy.

That may be a legitimate concern with institutional policies about trigger warnings. And yet, the problem with appeals to academic freedom in the debate over trigger warnings is that such appeals necessarily pit the rights of instructors against the rights of students. It's not uncommon for students requesting accommodations (even legally required accommodations) to be met with resistance and even outright refusal if their instructors feel the requests threaten their authority and academic freedom in the classroom (see, e.g., Flaherty 2017a). But for students, especially advocates of trigger warnings, the practice of academic freedom is inseparable from the accessibility of a class and its curriculum.[2]

Accessibility and Hospitality

Answering student requests for trigger warnings with appeals to academic freedom rhetorically positions the authority of the instructor as an ultimate good, even at the expense of students' ability to access the curriculum. At the same time, appeals to academic freedom first circulated in the trigger warnings debate then began recirculating in defense of injurious speech by nonmembers of the academy, including white supremacist reactionaries such as Milo Yiannopoulos and Richard Spencer. In this section, I argue that we should think of trigger warnings as a disability accommodation, one potential way of making college courses more accessible to students. But I also argue that inclusion can present us with contradictory ethical obligations, and I turn to the theory of hospitality to make sense of these contradictions. Accessibility can make the academy more hospitable, but hospitality always entails a risk.

Trigger warnings are an accessibility practice designed by and for people dealing with the aftermath of trauma. Being triggered is not the same thing as being asked to engage to material one finds objectionable, or even offensive, although some critics of trigger warnings have made that conflation. If a person is "triggered," they are experiencing an emotional or physical disruption in their cognitive process in response to a prior experience of trauma. Angela Carter, writing in *Disability Studies Quarterly* in 2015, explains that to be triggered means to "mentally and physically re-experience a past trauma in such an embodied manner that one's affective response literally takes over the ability to be present in one's bodymind." She describes common bodily symptoms of trauma that may impinge on a triggered person's ability to focus, let alone participate, in class, including the following: "hyperarousal such as increased heart rate, sweating, difficulty breathing, cold sweats, tingling, muscular tension; constriction of the nervous system and digestive system; dissociation and/or dysphoria; feeling numb, spacing out, or fully blacking out," as well as "hyper vigilance, sensitivity to light and sound, difficulty sleeping, a reduced capacity to manage stress and anxiety, amnesia and forgetfulness, chronic fatigue, immune system problems, headaches, and diminished ability to bond or connect with other individuals." In short, a triggered student is not in a state of mind or body conducive to learning.

When students request trigger warnings from their instructors, they are asking that their courses be made more accessible. Trigger warnings are designed to enable readers to prepare for the possibility of being triggered, and to take measures to reduce the disruption being triggered would cause. In their excellent theorization of trigger warnings as a community literacy practice, Sarah Orem and Neil Simpkins (2015) define trigger warnings as "textual tags attached to a variety of media that alert readers and viewers that the ensuing material could spur a mental health crisis." Their definition draws attention to the importance of mental health and disability communities to the emergence and circulation of trigger warnings.

Using trigger warnings does not eliminate the possibility that students may be triggered. Rather, they are a kind of information design, a tool that centers the needs of trauma survivors by enabling them to exercise some control over their own preparedness for encountering a known or likely trigger. Remi Yergeau (2014) argues that trigger warnings are a kind of "cripped metadata" because they anticipate the "embodied/enminded" response of a disabled audience, purposefully decentering the expectations of how a normatively abled audience ought to respond to our texts and our teaching. Other kinds of media "metadata" are hardly as heavily criticized as trigger warnings: think of motion picture ratings (which in the United States replaced the more regressive Hays Code), the use of blur or black boxes obstructing graphic images in news reports, or content descriptions that now commonly run before some episodes of TV shows, even on streaming services. While there are specific medical criteria that warrant thinking of trauma in terms of disability, there are also good reasons not to rely on institutional criteria alone in deciding how to make our courses accessible, not the least of which is that trauma can and does happen to students in the middle of our semesters, and that availing oneself of institutional support takes, among other resources, time.

Being triggered can be damaging for a student's mental and physical health, and students who are triggered might miss out on more than a single text, film, class period, or course in order to cope and recover. In a panel on trigger warnings at the 2016 MLA convention, then-assistant professor and writing program administrator Renea Frey said that the experience of being triggered in a course in college was so disruptive for her that she dropped out of school for two years. Trigger warnings are not the cause of students' intellectual disengagement from our classes; on the contrary, they provide one way for students to become better prepared and more deeply engaged. Some researchers have contested even this moderate claim, notably Jones, Bellet, and McNally (2020), who recruited participants from their introductory psychology courses and from Amazon's Mechanical Turk. Oddly, participants were given a partial list of clinical criteria with which to self-diagnose PTSD, and then were asked to rate the intensity of certain feelings (including anxiety, which was not clinically defined) after reading passages selected by the researchers. This context differs greatly from one in which students are being asked to discuss or write about a reading, and where a grade, and course credit, is at stake. The Jones et al. study garnered media attention both before and after its actual publication in 2020 (Gersen 2021; Khalid and Snyder 2021; Palus 2019), presumably because it purported to demonstrate that trigger warnings are "not helpful." But even this conclusion, if supported by the study, implies that an ideal reader would not experience any anxiety in response to reading, say, a graphically violent literary passage. The popular currency enjoyed by this type of psychological research on trigger warnings says a lot about the willingness to accept any other kind of evidence than what student survivors of trauma themselves have said about the issue.[3] Access to education is the opposite of shrinking from intellectual engagement. The accessibility of our curriculum is a prerequisite for ensuring that students with disabilities can fully participate in the classroom.

Teachers need to remember that trauma survivors can have not only divergent but at times *conflicting* needs, and that trigger warnings will not always be the right fit for every class or every group of students.[4] Survivors of sexual assault or domestic abuse may have different needs than military veterans or

Black students inundated with images of police violence against Black lives. But when students have conflicting needs, those conflicts have to be *negotiated*. If teachers do nothing, we are likely to reproduce the ambient norms of an academic culture that shuts out students dealing with trauma, disability, and mental illness (see Price 2001). Scholars and teachers who are committed to critical pedagogy ought to view the debate over trigger warnings as an opportunity to build solidarity with disabled people and disability studies scholars, and to make the academy more hospitable to people dealing with trauma.

Accessibility is a precondition for students' academic freedom. So how can we explain the use of academic freedom to block the accessibility requests of students? For this I turn to the theory of hospitality. Connecting many of the commonplaces against trigger warnings is the premise that students are outsiders to academic life, interlopers against a culture that students themselves are already saying is hostile to them. While faculty do have their reasons for feeling embattled, we cannot forget that some students are not at home in the university either. We ought to be reminded of this fact by students organizing against sexual violence on campuses, by hashtag campaigns like #BlackOn-Campus that create a space for students to bear witness to their lived experiences, and by student protests on a variety of issues aimed at making the university more hospitable—issues I take up in the subsequent chapters. Critiques of sensitive students try to close down the question of hospitality, territorializing the classroom as a space where freedom belongs to the instructor (only), and students are not to be welcomed, but to decrease their own resistance and obey authorities. In *Of Hospitality*, Jacques Derrida warns us, "One can become virtually xenophobic in order to protect or claim to protect one's own hospitality" (1997, 53). In defending our turf, we too easily become unable or unwilling to welcome our students, strangers though they may be, into the university. Following Derrida, we must observe that our defense of academic freedom and of the right to critique even violent norms is always at risk of becoming xenophobic, even in defense of our own hospitality.

The activism of students has been felt by some as an assault. Geoffrey Sirc gave this fear an epitomic image (back in 1993): "Student-desire as Godzilla, our curriculum as Tokyo" (210). Why are faculty so afraid that our own students will tear it all down? Thinking about our classrooms as spaces of hospitality can allow us to draw on a range of scholarly insights into the tensions between welcoming and belonging. Those of us who feel most at home in the academy may feel most deeply an obligation to protect it, and yet we're also obligated to welcome others who might transform it. As Jacqueline Jones Royster (1996) argues, welcoming strangers requires that any community's insiders be willing to "take high risk and give over the exclusivity of our rights to know" (33), particularly "as we go into classrooms and insist that our students trust us and what we contend is in their best interest" (38).

Derrida argues that strangers in need of hospitality are "first of all foreign to the legal language in which the duty of hospitality is formulated" (1997, 15). Strangers are forced to "ask for hospitality in a language which by definition is not [their] own, the one imposed on [them] by the master of the house, the host, the king, the lord, the authorities" (15), the teacher, the department chair, the dean. The university, too, is structured by relations of power. Students are to some extent foreigners to the university, and rhetoricians have long argued that students must be taught how to speak its language (see Bartholomae 1986; for more on the constraints mental health stigma places on rhetorical standing, see Johnson 2010; Pryal 2010; Rothfelder and Thornton 2017). If students who advocate for themselves turn first to the language of institutional requirements and policy for redress instead of to their instructors, perhaps they are against a wall that does not permit them to negotiate the norms by which class is conducted in any other language. Trigger warnings are one strategy that some students have adopted for making these norms explicit, negotiable, and consensual rather than tacit and reserved exclusively to the judgment of a teacher or institution. Margaret Price points out that instructors sometimes view student resistance against dominant norms as good "while also attempting to prevent resistance against the norms established in their own classrooms" (2001, 79). Yet such resistance is a sign that our students are searching for the language that might unlock our hospitality.

In the classroom, instructors have the best vantage point from which to welcome the differences and insights our students may bring. In an essay on disciplinary fights over correctness and style, Catherine Prendergast argues against the familiar apocalyptism of instructors convinced that their students will hasten the end of the academy as we know it. She urges teachers to attune ourselves to the places in "our own syllabi, writings, and in-class tangential rants where we are mourning stylistic or moral worlds gone by, and where we are spoiling for a fight to bring them back" (2009, 26)—a fitting description of the tenor of the trigger warnings debate. She continues: "Those fights mark those places where we reject what our students bring us, and what they have to offer us and one another (if we let them)" (26). In defense of our own academic freedom, we risk rejecting what our students have to contribute to the academy.

I have argued, on the one hand, that the sense of academic freedom circulating in the trigger warnings debate is narrow and inhospitable, and that it excludes issues of access. On the other hand, I turn now to a sense of academic freedom that's too broad. Commonplaces that pit sensitive students against academic freedom are also being deployed broadly to defend the espousal of repugnant views, especially by white supremacists, as (often paid) guests of the academy. Academic freedom is now being mobilized to protect and amplify reactionary hate speech, and to pretend that it has no material consequences.

To give but one example: In the year that preceded the 2017 implosion of former Breitbart tech editor Milo Yiannopoulos, recall that Yiannopoulos was marketed as an intellectual "provocateur," touring college campuses on the strength of his reputation inciting racist and misogynist harassment campaigns online. In December 2016, at the University of Wisconsin–Milwaukee, Yiannopoulos made disparaging sexual remarks about a trans student while displaying her photograph on-screen. He couched his remarks in an attack on Title IX. The university defended his speech as an opportunity for students to "hear diverse viewpoints" (Mone 2016).[5] The student, who with other protestors had warned administrators in advance about Yiannopoulos's history of targeted harassment, announced in a fiery open letter that she was quitting the university ("Hate's" 2016).

Do we really expect students who are exposed to this kind of attack by a guest speaker to simply grow a thicker skin? Or to attempt to engage in debate with someone whose worldview explicitly aims to incite violence and exclude them from existence? Driving a trans student out of her university is a victory for Yiannopoulos and his ilk. Let me underline that Yiannopoulos was a right-wing darling right up until the 2017 Conservative Political Action Conference dropped him as a speaker over the publicization of taped remarks he made about sex between men and boys (Peters, Alter, and Gynbaum 2017). His racism, misogyny, and targeted harassment of lesbians and trans women were publicized well before those taped remarks surfaced; in fact, they were his stock-in-trade. Yet he was welcomed to universities across the country because he was a critic of sensitive students. If we are so attached to an ideal of academic freedom that we choose to allow and amplify not only reckless but targeted hate speech meant to intimidate, provoke, and endanger our students, then we have let the fox into the henhouse. I am not denying the First Amendment right of even repugnant trolls to espouse their neo-Nazi ideology, but I am questioning whether the university ought to be giving it a platform completely divorced from the contexts of peer review and shared governance that legitimate academic freedom and make it possible for a field's experts to refute noxious and specious ideological claims. If universities protect and harbor hate speech outside of those vigorous contexts, we erode the doctrine of academic freedom and diminish the openness of higher education to students of all backgrounds.

We should be wary of appeals to academic freedom made in the service of reactionary political goals. Yet if hospitality requires us to welcome outsiders to the university as a part of our work as scholars (and I contend that it does), let there be no doubt that this work presents us with not only ethical questions but with occasions in which we must render ethical decisions. We are now and will continue to be confronted with occasions in which our obligation "to secure the space of academe as a sheltering place of unconditional hospitality for dissidence and insurrection, refutation and un-domesticatable explosions of thought" (Ronell quoted in Davis 2000, 248)[6] nevertheless demands that we decide between mutually exclusive alternatives. Do we protect the trans student Yiannopoulos targeted, or do we promote Yiannopoulos's sexually harassing remarks, couched in critique of sexual harassment policy, as a diverse and valid viewpoint? Do we protect our students (and faculty and staff) of color, or do we promote the injurious speech of white supremacists? To whom does our hospitality extend when we are faced with mutually exclusive alternatives? These are not hypothetical questions.

It is sensitive students who are opening up this ethical scene, making it visible to their peers and teachers and scholars. How do we secure the space of the university and protect its capacity to shelter this sensitivity while at the same time taking care not to become xenophobic in our defense? Derrida argues that the necessity of rendering decisions in no way releases us from the unconditionality of these contradictory obligations. Hospitality is only possible because of its productive internal contradiction: the ability to welcome strangers depends on the authority to close one's home to strangers. Turning hospitality's unconditionality against itself is structurally impossible to prevent. But if we refuse to turn to particulars, Derrida says the concept of hospitality will be "abstract, utopian, illusory," in danger of becoming its own opposite (1997, 79). "It wouldn't be effectively unconditional," Derrida insists, "if it didn't *have to become* effective, concrete, determined" (79). Hospitality provides us with an obligation, but not with principles about how this obligation is to be satisfied. If the boundaries we are willing to assign to academic freedom endanger the vulnerable and protect the powerful, then, like hospitality, it becomes abstract, utopian, and illusory.

Applying the theory of hospitality to accessibility and academic freedom enables us to see inclusion as an ethical problem, not a simple imperative to bring outsiders in. The view that accessibility and academic freedom are competing interests is inhospitable, and it has become an ideological premise for reactionary political attacks on sensitive students and on the university as an intellectual home. But I can't prescribe a master set of best practices for making every classroom more hospitable because the particulars of hospitality must constantly be revisited. When a student asks for trigger warnings, they risk exposing their own vulnerability; for example, a student asking for trigger warnings about sexual violence may expose that student as a survivor (for more on the relationship between access and disclosure, see Kafer 2016). For this reason, I believe that any policy on using trigger warnings should be negotiated together by a particular class of students and not imposed administratively. What I can say is that instructors who spend some class time discussing how potentially triggering course material ought to be handled, or even who write a few sentences on this question into their syllabi's accessibility statements, may be more successful at welcoming students who are living with trauma into the university.

The theoretical issues at stake in the trigger warnings debate go beyond the vulnerability of sensitive students. As rhetoricians, we are positioned to observe what this debate has to teach us about the capacity of language to do harm, violence, and trauma. Trigger warnings don't just expose the sensitivity of individual students; they also expose a *shared* sensitivity, a mutual exposedness to affection and even trauma in language. This exposedness marks the site of a "rhetorical trauma"—that is to say, an openness to being affected in language that has been criticized as (over-)sensitivity.

Rhetorical Trauma

If as a child you learned the rhyme, "Sticks and stones may break my bones, but words will never hurt me," you were learning to contrast the harm that language can do with the harm of physical violence, and to minimize the effectivity of words to do violence. But words—and images and symbols—can and do hurt. Eve Sedgwick (2003), Judith Butler (1997, 2005), Jacques Derrida (1997)—even the ancient Sophist Gorgias (1972) argued that language has intoxicating powers, operating behind and *before* the discriminating faculties of conscious volition. Diane Davis (2010) contends that the power of language to instantiate, as well as to move, or to wound, comes from our relation to language—our rhetoricity. Rhetoricity names an "affect*ability* or persuad*ability*" (2; emphasis in original) that makes symbolic action possible. Although Davis emphasizes *ability* in this gloss of rhetoricity, she demonstrates that rhetoricity is not the kind of relation that rhetorical subjects can simply opt into or out of. On the contrary, rhetoricity is constitutive of agency and of subjectivity, and even of relationality itself. To be addressed and affected, to be able to respond, and to be able to become a rhetorical subject, we must somehow be vulnerable, exposed, or open to the affection of address from outside ourselves. Words can hurt not only because they can affect us but because we *cannot stop them* from affecting us. The affection of language always pierces us. Because we can neither limit nor control our own exposedness, rhetorical affection can be traumatic, interrupting one's capacity to make meaning and to experience oneself as an agentive rhetorical subject.

I am positioning *sensitivity* here as a rhetorical term adjacent to rhetoricity in order to emphasize that rhetoricity does not describe an ability, capacity, or power. Sensitivity, like rhetoricity, is rather an incapacity or inability to stop oneself from being affected in language. The rhetorical structure that exposes us to an/other's address and affection is not one we can exit when we get tired, overwhelmed, or even injured, no more than we can shut off the receptivity of our olfactory senses to the possible presence of scents. We can *maybe* hold our noses and block up the channel, but the necessity of doing so demonstrates the existence of a passage connecting and exposing our interiority to everything outside. Sensitivity names a structural opening into (and prior to) the subject through which language—affection from exteriority—may enter, not against our will but before it. The sensitivity of the rhetorical subject is what actually makes it possible for the subject to both receive and respond to that which affects us. And this sensitivity can't be simply stopped, shut off, laughed off, or grown out of—no matter what critics of sensitive students have claimed. Language wounds and opens us all.

I don't mean to claim that all rhetorical *action* is necessarily violent, or that rhetoric doesn't also enable its subjects to exercise power or agency and to experience rhetorical affection as positive and empowering, as joy, or even as jouissance.[7] But the power of language to wound is one and the same as its power to open; we can no more control our sensitivity in and to the pleasures of language than we can control our sensitivity in and to its injuries. So that even when the affection of language is a delight, this too depends on our prior inability, incapacity, and nonpower—on our prior sensitivity. Rhetorical affection is at this level *always* traumatic, because no rhetorical subject can stop it from happening. It constitutes us; it precedes and exceeds us. Even when we cannot make sense of this rhetorical affection, we are nevertheless obligated to respond to it.

Some may object to characterizing the harm done by and through language in terms of trauma and violence. In Sarah Schulman's 2016 *Conflict Is Not Abuse*, in a section on trigger warnings, she argues that "the word 'violence' should be used to describe physical violence" in order to avoid "exploiting the rhetoric of victimization" (92). She views *violence* in usages like mine as metaphorical—"rhetorical devices that hide details [and] keep truth from being known and faced" (93). Obviously I disagree. Schulman's justification for this claim presupposes that harm done by and through language is fake, whereas physical violence is real. This presupposition rests on imagining rhetorical subjects as hermetically sealed, properly insensitive to affection in language— not actually rhetorical at all. Schulman's wariness of the "rhetoric of victimization" is part of a larger argument for reframing some claims of abuse in terms of conflict, where there is no perpetrator and no victim, only "conflicted" parties. The problem that Schulman admits but does not solve is that instances of abuse do exist, often in circumstances where one party exploits their power over another (purposefully or not). Violence can happen without the striking of a single physical blow. The usage of "violence" to describe such instances may not be physical, but that does not make it less literal.

Schulman is not the only queer feminist scholar who has recirculated commonplaces against sensitive students. In an essay in the Feminist Key Concepts and Controversies series in *Signs*, Jack Halberstam argues that trigger warnings position "the student as a fragile organism with no intellectual immune system" and as "a defenseless, passive, and inert spectator who has no barriers between herself and the flow of images that populate her world" (2017, 539, 541). What's assumed here is that trigger warnings will not be used for access but for insulation from intellectual engagement; that sensitive students, unable to perform the self-protective (and, we should observe, life-sustaining) function of an "intellectual immune system" for themselves, want faculty and administrators to perform that function for them. The essay concludes with this call to action: "We must oppose the trigger warning . . . because it gives rise to an understanding of self that makes us vulnerable to paternalistic modes of protection" (541). Halberstam's argument here is that accepting a view of rhetorical subjects as sensitive or vulnerable *is itself* what renders us vulnerable.

Halberstam's *Signs* article is one of the few entries in the debate against trigger warnings that bothers to address the pedagogical issues at stake. Halberstam argues for the pedagogical value of exposing students to shocking images in certain contexts (e.g., a class about the Holocaust). Surprising students with not only difficult but traumatic images and texts probably should not be a routine part of pedagogical strategy, and we need not accept the premise that offering students a trigger warning undercuts the shocking force of such texts or images. Ann Cvetkovich explains that when "the representation of suffering is presumed to have a salutary effect on an audience," the audience is presumed to be "removed culturally and geographically" from that suffering, and the representation itself is presumed to be transparent rather than rhetorical (2012, 9). Some critics argue that the normal procedures of their classrooms would be disrupted if they had to warn their students about possible triggers (7 Humanities Professors 2014). This claim implies that the potential for trauma is so regularly inflicted on students that to advise them about it in advance would halt the day-to-day activities of teaching. If trigger warnings would be disruptive of one's normal teaching, the underlying premise is that such teaching is traumatic. Presumably, critics would prefer to teach appropriately insensitive students, students who would submit to their instructors' will to shock them, somehow without being wounded, pierced, or affected, even by texts and images expressly intended to wound, pierce, and affect.[8]

Trigger warnings are a way of acknowledging the fact that language and representation can and do touch us in traumatic ways. They acknowledge our inability to stop ourselves from suffering, from undergoing affection in language. An acknowledgment like this can be sensitizing: it can make students and teachers more aware of their own vulnerabilities but also of the rhetorical power we wield and its capacity to harm others. Trigger warnings do nothing to coddle or insulate students from the trauma of rhetorical affection—on the contrary, they are precisely one way of opening up to it. Sensitivity opens one toward trauma instead of shutting down and closing oneself off from it. Of course, trigger warnings are not a way of guaranteeing that no one will undergo the "re-traumatization" of being triggered, which is to say that no one can altogether avoid or opt out of trauma's aftermath (Carter 2015). Still, trigger warnings can sometimes help students prepare to face known triggers. At the very least, they offer teachers a way to signal that there might be trauma ahead. Some critics claim that this signaling trains students to respond *as if* they have been traumatized (Filipovic 2014; Kipnis 2015a). My point is teachers who talk about whether and how to use trigger warnings with their students have an opportunity to teach their students about how to respond to rhetorical trauma that teachers who don't, well, don't.

That ability to respond is a crucial rhetorical skill, which means it is absolutely within the purview of teachers and scholars of writing, communication, and language. I am not saying that we are equipped by our training to handle mental health crises in (or as a result of) our classrooms—only that we should not be shocked or insulted to learn from our students that such crises can and do occur. We do have an expert vantage on the rhetorical force of language and on how and why language can be destabilizing, and a responsibility to our students attends this expertise (see Bishop 1993). But it's not just our sensitive students: we are *all* vulnerable to and even defenseless against the trauma that is rhetorical affection, the fact that language does wound and open us all, and anyone can touch us with an address, be they a teacher, a student, a campus preacher, a friend, an intimate, or a stranger. The fact that we can be affected with language is the sign of a prior rhetorical sensitivity that brings us into relation with one another as rhetorical subjects. We are exposed to one another without protection in a fundamentally rhetorical relation, open to being addressed in language, and we are always affected by that address, and even by its very possibility. Sensitivity to rhetorical trauma gives us our response/ability, and with it, a responsibility *to respond*. Rhetorical sensitivity is traumatic because our exposedness is not something we can control, turning it on when we're ready and off when we're overloaded. Sensitivity overwhelms cognition, ruptures experience, and exceeds our ability to make it meaningful: it is a condition of possibility for both receiving and responding to rhetorical affection. On this view, trauma is something that no one can be simply shielded from, but something that all of us must (and do) respond to. It is also precisely what makes learning possible.

Trauma is an important lens for thinking about what happens in the classroom. In their "Presence in Absence: Discourses and Teaching (in, on, and about) Trauma," Peter N. Goggin and Maureen Daly Goggin (2005) contend that the discourse of trauma "can serve to illuminate the shadowy aspects of safety and community that are often (and naively) presumed in the writing class" (39). They argue that "the classroom is *not* a safe place" because it can never be "hermetically sealed off from the world in which it is situated" (39). The classroom is immersed in the same relations of power and vulnerability as the world. Daphne Read (1998) argues that especially in higher education, "there is a deep reluctance to deal with . . . trauma as students experience it" (111). There's an assumption that "trauma 'belongs' in the texts we study, not in the texts students write" (111)—and I'll add, certainly not in the lives of our students. Learning itself is traumatic: learning differs in this way from simply adding to what one already knows. "If it's really learning," Davis writes, following Levinas, "then it is necessarily a trauma" (2010, 74). Learning doesn't have to be *hurtful*—but it has to exceed our preexisting structures of understanding. Appropriating our experiences to these structures may add to what we know, but knowing is different than learning. In *Totality and Infinity*, Levinas argues that teaching is something other than the transport of ideas from latency into the clear light of consciousness. For him, "teaching . . . comes from the exterior and brings me more than I contain" (1961, 51). It exceeds what the mind can already grasp and make sense of. In the Lacanian variant of this case for the link between learning and trauma, the scene of pedagogy is fraught with relations of power, authority, desire, and resistance (see Alcorn 2002; Felman 1982). What makes learning traumatic is that learning requires a *failure* of understanding and an *inability* to grasp, a rupture of what is already known that makes way for learning something different.

Trauma of this kind *is* disorienting: Davis calls it "a shattering of self and world" (2010, 74). It is impossible to skirt the ethical implication. There is trauma in our rhetorical sensitivity, in this possibility of being addressed and affected in a way that is inappropriable to meaning, and teachers and their students are always implicated in precisely this rhetorical relation. Pedagogy involves a rhetorical trauma or violence from which we cannot simply absolve ourselves. Perhaps we should be (more) anxious about this ordinary violence involved in exposing students to difficult and traumatic material—which is not to say we should not teach it. But triggered students are left stranded in this disorientation. And, as rhetoricians have aimed to demonstrate for millennia, teaching is the possibility of beginning to reorganize, respond, and instantiate both self and world differently.

Toward a More Sensitive Rhetoric

Sensitivity describes a condition of possibility for rhetorical action. It comes before the exercise of symbolism and the generation of shared meaning, before persuasion and identification. The rhetoricity of rhetorical subjects is their condition of being exposed—*sensitive*—to the trauma of rhetorical affection. Critics who denigrate and disavow sensitivity engage in the construction of a fantasy subject, one who is closed off, unfeeling or at least unfailingly appropriate in what they feel, insensitive to the trauma of being addressed. Such a subject could never be moved or touched: no shock, no violence, no affection of any kind could pierce the borders of a subject without sensitivity. Being sensitive means being *unable* to stop oneself from being addressed, and *unable* to close oneself against the trauma of rhetorical affection. Nothing could touch the rhetorical subject unless it can also be touched in language; unless, in fact, *first of all*, it can do nothing to shield itself from rhetorical affection; unless we are, first of all, sensitive.

Repudiating the sensitivity of the rhetorical subject functions as a way of absolving the critic of the violence of their own address, as if one could simply opt out of the space of ethical decision opened by teaching when learning is (necessarily) traumatic. Through its disavowal, sensitivity has become the center of public discussion about harm, trauma, feeling, and responsibility in the scene of the college campus. Even the denigration of sensitivity is already a response to the mutuality of our exposedness to rhetorical affection. If it cannot be quashed, sensitivity can at least be buried or obscured, and it often is, by circuits of social and institutional power. While it is certainly possible to regulate and punish those uses of language that offend, it is not really possible to threaten the *rhetorical* relation that makes hurt or harm possible. Sensitivity can be denigrated and disavowed, but it is never really possible to sever the connection we have to each other in language by virtue of our exposedness to address. For Davis, our very exposedness forms the basis for solidarity: what is shared among rhetorical existents is not an essential commonality but our "irreparable openness to affection/alteration" (2010, 4).

In the domain of rhetorical theory, my argument aims to resignify sensitivity as a route into and through the rhetorical subject, not a weakness or moral failing but a condition of one's constitution in language. This writing, then, can be read as an exposition of rhetorical exposedness, one answer to Davis's call for rhetorical scholarship that does the ceaseless work of "excavating, examining, and affirming the saying *as* rhetoric, as an extra-symbolic rhetorical appeal" (2010, 17). I aim to open a dehiscence in the common sense of the community regarding trigger warnings. "Dehiscence" names a rupturing open; it's usually used to describe either a blossom or a wound. There is perhaps an indeterminable relation between those two alternatives: what bears fruit may also injure; what pierces one's defenses may also germinate and thrive.

In *Living a Feminist Life* (2017), Sara Ahmed observes, "the moral panic over trigger warnings often evokes this figure . . . of the oversensitive student who is not attuned to the difficulty and discomfort of learning, as if to say: if we let your sensitivities become law, we lose our freedom" (262). My argument flips the claim Ahmed attributes to critics of trigger warnings here. Sensitive students are attuned precisely to the difficulty and discomfort of learning (and are looking for ways to face it). Their critics are not. In Ahmed's analysis, "freedom has become reduced to the freedom to be offensive, which is also about how those with power protect their right to articulate their own views, no matter what" (262). No matter the harm. We ought to stop circulating arguments that depend on the repudiation of sensitivity, and we ought to counter them effectively wherever they continue to appear. In a blog post on trigger warnings, Andrea Lunsford notes that writing teachers "have a real advantage in terms of getting to know our students: we are likely to know when and if trigger warnings would be beneficial" (Lunsford 2016). I agree conditions are favorable in smaller classes where instructors are reading student writing or otherwise responding to student texts, but the work of hospitality and of welcoming difference within our institutions will be difficult work, work that demands our response even to the undecidable questions it presents us with.

Lunsford (2016) observes: "We remember—even if those embroiled in the current discussion do not—the culture wars and Mary Louise Pratt's important elaboration of what she called the 'contact zone' and its corollary, the safe house." Pratt's 1991 article argues that contact zones are "social spaces where cultures meet, clash, and grapple with each other" (34). She defines this key term in part against the prevailing view of a classroom "community" in which "discrete, self-defined, coherent entities" are held together by equal shares of literacy in a shared language or set of goals and rules (38). Students' literacies differ, defer, and diverge. Pratt argues that students' interests are often effaced by the institutional authority of teachers. If we want our classrooms to be contact zones, according to Pratt, we cannot forget that students (or anyone entering the contact zone) *also need* what Pratt's students called "safe houses"—"intellectual spaces where groups can constitute themselves . . . with high degrees of trust, shared understandings, [and] temporary protection from legacies of oppression" (40).[9] As Ahmed suggests, "student movements might be teaching us how attending to fragility, the histories that render some more fragile than others, can be a source of militancy" (2017, 239). Understanding that the safe house is a precondition for the contact zone—and that sensitivity is the precondition for rhetorical affection—should change the way we think and argue about trigger warnings and other issues of academic freedom and free speech on campus where figures of "sensitive students" are likely to appear.

Ideology tends to change slowly, but arguments in defense of sensitivity have begun to become hearable (see, e.g., Baer 2017, 2019). I hope the defense and reclamation of sensitivity in this book will accelerate the breakup of the common sense against sensitivity, which has prevented us from being able to recognize and receive the insights of our students, and which moreover has denied us opportunities to discuss with them (and each other) the rhetorical predicament that opens us to one another. A more sensitive rhetoric would affirm the priority of exposedness to alterity in the formation of rhetorical subjects, as well as the responsibility to respond engendered in this preoriginary scene of trauma and nonpower. A more sensitive rhetoric would seek out ways of teaching and persuading that equips students with the rhetorical resources to respond, even to difficult, painful, or traumatic texts. Sensitivity marks the place where widely held commonplaces converge with theory about rhetoric and affection in language. A rhetorical theory of sensitivity can demonstrate the extraordinary force of the irrepressible rhetorical relation.

This chapter has demonstrated the intervention that sensitive rhetorics can make in practical policy debates by surfacing the rhetorical consequences of how the trigger warnings debate has been argued. Well after "The Year of the Trigger Warning," the issues and premises invoked in the debate over their use in college classes found their way into similarly argued debates over other campus activist issues. Yet sensitivity is a precondition for the rhetorical affection on which teaching and learning depend. In the next chapter, I turn my attention to the rhetorically related debate over another campus issue: Title IX and sexual misconduct policy. Sensitivity has also appeared as a trope in debates about the scope and enforcement of Title IX's application to sexual assault and sexual harassment, especially at colleges and universities. Critics of Title IX span the political spectrum, from feminist scholar Laura Kipnis to former Secretary of Education Betsy DeVos. Rhetorically, these critics are united by their expression of concern for the due process rights of the accused, and accusations of sensitivity invoke other premises about the meaning and function of sexual harassment. Feminist critics like Kipnis also express concern over the construction of sexuality as legally fraught and of women especially as fragile victims who lack sexual agency. The next chapter argues that critiques of sensitivity misrepresent or misunderstand student activists' arguments that sexual harassment is a form of institutional power. I argue that an institutional rhetoric of sensitivity can help us understand the legal, financial, and ethical relations of the university as themselves structured by exposure.

Chapter 2

Sensitive Subjects

Sexual Misconduct Policy and Sexual Power

Title IX is meant to address a toxic, abusive set of actions as they unfold within a sexist social structure. Each crisis, as it is administered, is individuated. And yet each crisis vibrates with the largest and deepest of existing structural flaws.

Jennifer Doyle, *Campus Sex, Campus Security*

In the previous chapter, I showed how claims about sensitivity functioned in the trigger warnings debate as a proxy for claims about rhetorical power and vulnerability in language. In this chapter, I turn to the debate over Title IX, a closely related campus activist issue, and one that, like trigger warnings, is also shot through with the political and pedagogical relations that obtain between teachers and students, as well as administrators and activists. Title IX of the Education Amendments Act of 1972 is the legal framework for sexual harassment law in US American universities, colleges, and schools. This chapter examines how critiques of sensitivity are circulated in debates over Title IX: once again, how they attach to appeals to academic freedom on the part of the faculty, and how they are used to undermine student activists and exclude them from policy conversations. And while policy can function to insulate institutions from vulnerability, sensitivity nevertheless underwrites the structuring relations of the university.

When I began my research on trigger warnings, which was the genesis of this project as a book, I tuned in to the way feelings and affect and specifically sensitivity were being talked about in the trigger warnings debate. Accusations that students were "just being too sensitive" were used to erode the rhetorical authority that students brought to the policy discussion, a discussion that should have been and still ought to be about accessibility, about coping with and recovering from trauma, and about obligations that college and university instructors—and the institutions that appoint and authorize us—have to our students. The figure of the sexual assault survivor was at once everywhere and nowhere in these conversations. The traumatized student was often spoken or written about as if she was a white middle class woman endangered by her living at a residential college.[1] Critics of trigger warnings sometimes called attention to the way this figure of a young white woman could work to occlude other kinds of student trauma, including the structural, racial trauma of Black students or the trauma of working-class students staving off poverty. And yet, these critics themselves rarely named (let alone wrote or spoke) of rape.

Building on my discussion of rhetorical trauma in the previous chapter, I want to begin this chapter by acknowledging the structuring character of sexual violence in US American culture (see Larson 2021; Vitanza 2011) and in US American universities (e.g., a 2014 report found that fewer than one-third of students found responsible for sexual assault were expelled, and fewer than half were suspended, Kingkade 2014; see also Cantor, Fisher, and Chiball et al. 2017; Krebs, Lindquist, and Warner et al. 2007; Smith and Freyd 2013). What I want to analyze, though, is how the fantasy (as in, the ideologically controlling image) of "the rape victim" (as if there is only one) both structures the debate over Title IX policies and nevertheless evades the central issues and questions that shape it. I have chosen to focus my analysis more on sexual harassment than on sexual assault here because, although sexual harassment can and certainly often does involve physical transgressions, sexual harassment may at least in theory take place only and exclusively in language.[2] Part of what I hope to demonstrate is the instability of the boundary that confines sexual harassment to language alone; the corollary would be that sexual violence may not be confined to physical transgression alone, either.

Like the trigger warnings debate, debates over Title IX policies have no shortage of accusations that students are being too sensitive. Something that piqued my interest in these debates was that even queer and feminist scholars—people who were otherwise critical of exclusionary academic norms—were echoing the claims of reactionary and often conservative critics of higher education. What they shared most intensely was a critique of students' sensitivity. My analysis of the beliefs and values attached to these critiques showed me that casting students' sensitivity as a threat to academic freedom has been a highly resonant appeal, one that moved a broad audience to accept arguments that construct students as neoliberal consumers rather than activists advocating for their own access, safety, and well-being in the university. The argument I advance here by focusing on Title IX specifically is that even feminist critics of Title IX who accuse student activists of being too sensitive are disavowing the constitutive rhetorical exposedness that makes both education and ethics possible.

Building on the claim of the previous chapter that sensitivity is the condition of possibility for rhetorical relationships, I contend in this chapter that not only students and faculty but institutions, too, can be sensitive. I first offer a brief history of Title IX, and how discrimination on the basis of sex has come to include both sexual harassment and sexual assault. Sometimes these two categories are referred to together as "sexual misconduct," but confoundingly sometimes "sexual misconduct" is used to refer to behavior that is not deemed either severe or pervasive enough to count as harassment. Critics of student activists have exploited this equivocation. Feminist scholars such as Laura Kipnis have linked their critiques of student activists to appeals to academic freedom in a rhetorical move that ignores the work of student activists and advocates of Title IX in critiquing sexual power in institutions of higher education. I conclude by calling for a theory of rhetoric informed by sensitivity, and by saying a bit about how I see sensitive rhetorics shaping disciplinary conversations about ethics, rhetorical agency, and the capacity of language to do harm.

A Recent History of Title IX Policy

Title IX of the Education Amendments Act of 1972 prohibits discrimination on the basis of sex in schools that receive public funding. The text of the law reads: "No person in the United States shall, on the basis of sex, be excluded from participation in, be denied the benefits of, or be subjected to discrimination under any education program or activity receiving Federal financial assistance." In the late 1970s and early 1980s, feminist legal scholar Catharine MacKinnon became the architect of a legal framework that positioned sexual harassment at work and at school as a form of sex discrimination. MacKinnon is often figured in recent memory as a conservative relic of the feminist sex wars because of her high-profile campaign to pass city ordinances defining pornography as a form of sex discrimination. MacKinnon's hometown of Minneapolis hired her and frequent collaborator Andrea Dworkin as consultants to help pass the ordinance twice, but it was vetoed both times by the mayor. Courts struck these ordinances down in the handful of other cities that passed them. But MacKinnon's legal framework construing sexual harassment as sex discrimination has been extremely influential, and courts affirmed it in Title IX cases several times in the 1990s.

In her introduction to a recent interview with MacKinnon published in *Signs*, Durba Mitra describes MacKinnon as "one of the most cited legal scholars in the English language" (Mitra and MacKinnon 2018). Her book *Sexual Harassment of Working Women: A Case of Sex Discrimination* was published in 1979; in 1980, the Second Circuit accepted MacKinnon's argument that sexual harassment could constitute sex discrimination in an educational setting; and in 1986, MacKinnon prevailed as co-counsel before the Supreme Court in *Meritor Savings Bank v. Vinson*, which established that a claim of sexual harassment may be based on a hostile work environment, and that sexual conduct may contribute to such an environment if it is unwelcome. MacKinnon's legal framework for linking sexual harassment to sex discrimination was doubtlessly groundbreaking, but it installed contradictions in the law and theory of sexual harassment that are irresolvable. These contradictions, and the long-simmering tensions embedded in the theories of sexual harassment that the law has produced, are carefully exposed in Elizabeth Anderson's (2006) review of a collection of essays coedited by MacKinnon and Riva Siegel (2004). Anderson argues that literature on sexual harassment tends to address itself to either (1) identifying the harms of sexual harassment and what makes it a normative wrong, (2) identifying the causes of sexual harassment and how it can be decreased, or (3) identifying legal avenues for complaint and redress. But Anderson contends that these aims are sometimes in conflict, and different foci will produce differences in theory.

Anderson (2006) names three broad approaches to accounting for sexual harassment: *dignity* theory, *autonomy* theory, and *equality* theory. Dignity theories focus on the intrinsic harm of humiliation sustained by targets of harassment—as a result, dignity theories might miss or obscure the sexual character of power involved in sexual harassment, or even tend to moralize about the inappropriateness of sexuality as such. Autonomy theories may be more welcoming to the publicity of sexuality, focusing on the violation of the will of targets of sexual harassment. The relevant question for autonomy theories becomes which advances are actually unwelcome. Equality theories, like MacKinnon's, are grounded in disparate treatment of the sexes, which implies that men are not subject to sexual harassment, at least in the same way that women are (i.e., as a class). Under an equality theory, the harms suffered by targets of harassment need not always be individual or emotional, because the harms are always material and suffered as a class. It's worth noting that in Anderson's view, the spreading and somewhat patchwork legal framework of sexual harassment law might be better addressed by "alternative laws aimed at securing the dignity and autonomy of workers and students"—she contends this approach "would offer more coherent and comprehensive remedies for some wrongs now alleged to constitute sex discrimination" (289; see also Hill and Stabile 2021 for more on sexual harassment as a labor issue in higher ed). Title IX case law and administrative law as we know it bundles the tensions and contradictions of these conflicting theoretical approaches and aims (see also Fernandez, Lawrence, and Stabile 2020).

A recent era of controversy over Title IX came about in the wake of the Obama administration's 2011 Dear Colleague Letter, sometimes called the DCL. The DCL is essentially a memo issued by the Department of Education's Office for Civil Rights, and it instructed universities to follow certain procedures for investigating Title IX complaints about both sexual harassment and sexual assault. Among these was the prescription that Title IX investigations employ a "preponderance of the evidence" standard, which is the standard of evidence used in civil rights cases, and which is rhetorically consonant with the MacKinnonite view that sex discrimination violates the civil rights of women. Critics of the DCL have pointed to this requirement as a key component of what they view as the excesses of Title IX, claiming that the policy violates the due process rights of the accused (see, e.g., Gersen and Suk 2016; Gertner 2015; Halley 2015). But Title IX investigations are not criminal, nor are they civil legal proceedings. They are administrative compliance procedures that are set up to shield the university from liability exposure, from complainants, and from the government. And, before 2011, some 80% of schools with a fixed standard of evidence for Title IX investigations *already used* the preponderance standard, while most of the rest used "clear and convincing," a slightly higher standard (Joyce 2017).

Although Title IX processes differ at different universities, they usually follow this pattern: a report reaches the Title IX officer, who initiates an investigation, conducts interviews with relevant parties, and writes a report that both complainant and respondent may review and comment on before a university hearing. Often a panel composed of university faculty, staff, and students presides at the hearing and issues findings of responsibility, unless the evidence is deemed insufficient. Punishment may be recommended by the panel but is usually determined by higher-level administrators. Some universities designate an officer to hear appeals; at others, appeals can go as high as the university president.

These procedures are Byzantine. And this is a *generalized* description; institutional variation can alter the process substantially (see Porter, Levitsky, and Armstrong 2023 for a national study of procedural variations). After six years of Title IX policy governed by the DCL, Trump administration Secretary of Education Betsy DeVos rescinded the DCL in September 2017. New rules were proposed in November 2018, and despite the submission of more than a hundred thousand public comments in the scant two months of public comment period, the new rules were formalized as administrative law (Chu and Lewis 2019; Czajka 2019; Meckler 2018). The DeVos rules ended the standard of evidence requirement (allowing schools to set a much higher standard, which advantages respondents), circumscribed the authority of schools to investigate incidents that take place off campus (at, say, apartments or house parties), allowed mediation as an alternative to the Title IX investigation process, and permitted cross-examination of complainants by respondents (and vice versa). The rules also raised the threshold for institutional liability, substantially lessening pressure on schools to prevent sexual harassment and assault—universities are only considered liable when a school official, having "actual knowledge" of a violation, shows "deliberate indifference" in their response (Brown and Mangan 2018; Green 2018). So I suppose indifference that's unconscious or unintentional is permissible.[3]

Perhaps critics of Title IX got more than they bargained for. It's worth noting that while critics construe the law as extremely powerful, it is also quite vulnerable to the vicissitudes of the executive tasked with its enforcement. Halfway through President Trump's second year in office, *Inside Higher Ed* reported an 11% reduction in staff in the Department of Education's Office for Civil Rights, or OCR, led at the time by Deputy Assistant Secretary Candice Jackson (Kreighbaum 2018). Seventy staff members had left and not been replaced in the previous year. The OCR, which is the office that issued the 2011 DCL, is responsible for investigating discrimination complaints—sex discrimination as well as discrimination based on race or disability. The Trump administration's inability or unwillingness to staff the OCR reflects the goal of weakening Title IX and undermining its enforcement mechanisms. The Biden administration telegraphed their own rules change at the end of 2021, which then underwent a similar public comment period (US Department of Education 2021). In the meantime, students continue to navigate sexual misconduct and discrimination claims under the DeVos rules.

Sexual Misconduct and the Scope of Sex Discrimination

News headlines have tended to refer to both the DCL and the DeVos rules as "sexual misconduct" rules, which for a headline editor seems to be a way of saving the space required to write "sexual harassment and sexual assault" (SHSA). But at some institutions, policies such as student or faculty codes of conduct also define sexual misconduct as prohibited and punishable behavior, even if it would not satisfy the criteria for a Title IX violation—which, remember, is discrimination. MacKinnon writes in her article "In Their Hands: Restoring Institutional Liability for Sexual Harassment in Education" that her "suspicion is that the substitution of 'sexual misconduct' for sexual harassment in some school policies is, at least in part, an attempt to dodge legal accountability, as no judicial standards exist to which schools are held in their treatment of 'sexual misconduct' per se" (2016, 2042). Sexual misconduct legally should be understood to be discriminatory if it involves either an explicit quid pro quo or if it creates a hostile environment. To qualify as hostile environment harassment, sexual misconduct must be deemed either severe or pervasive enough to disrupt a complainant's equal access to education. The MacKinnonite feminist viewpoint holds that this is the ideological *point* of sexual harassment and sexual assault on campus: to intimidate and harm women in a way that damages their education.

And yet, since the era of the feminist sex wars, and perhaps even since the 2011 issuance of the DCL, what counts as discrimination on the basis of sex has expanded, albeit in a patchwork way. Male students are also vulnerable to assault and harassment (as illustrated at least partially by the high profile of the 2018 Title IX complaint and finding of sexual harassment against Avital Ronell[4]). Queer, trans, and gender-nonconforming students are exposed to assault and harassment, including at school, at much higher rates than straight and cisgender peers—*and* they are rhetorically positioned as likely threats rather than likely victims, *even and especially under Title IX*, a policy that once protected their rights. The DCL is not the only Obama-era Title IX guidance DeVos rescinded: she also rescinded guidance that ensured trans students would be allowed to use bathrooms and locker rooms appropriate to their gender at school. The definition of discrimination on the basis of sex has expanded, but, let me underline, it's also in a state of flux.

And at least to some extent, its expansion may have the effect of *de-gendering* (or unsexing) sex discrimination, since people of all genders may be subjected to sexual harassment. Yet students are most often the vulnerable parties in the context of higher education, even when their harassers are also students. The proposition that male students are discriminated against on the basis of their sex is a claim that critics of Title IX have actually hewed to, and even tried to advance in the courts in cases where male respondents—that is, students who were accused of sexual harassment or assault—were found responsible by their institutions' Title IX proceedings and then turned around and sued their schools. Title IX scholar Erin Buzuvis published a thorough review of such lawsuits in 2017, contending that the increased filing of such suits is not an effect of the DCL, or at least, not its procedures, but of increased investigation and enforcement. Critics say that the DCL made men vulnerable to false accusations to the point of discriminating against men (a premise that was loudly echoed in the wider public discussion of the #MeToo movement and in the wake of Christine Blasey Ford's testimony in the 2018 confirmation hearing of Supreme Court Justice Brett Kavanaugh). But as Buzuvis notes, "The majority of [Title IX] disciplinary proceedings do not find respondents responsible" and, in fact, "less than half of respondents who are found responsible for sexual assault are expelled" (2017, 71). Less than half of those *found responsible* are expelled. Courts have tended to agree with Buzuvis's assessment, rejecting the idea that Title IX discriminates against men, even in those instances where evidence of a bias against Title IX *respondents* (who aren't always men) is presented (90).

To be sure, sexual harassment can be used to target people of any gender, as well as any rank or professional status, and while students are not the only people targeted by sexual harassment in higher education (see again Hill and Stabile 2021), it is student activists and advocacy groups who have most visibly focused their efforts and resources on strengthening Title IX, including by mounting collective challenges to the DeVos rules in court. And it is student activists and advocates who have drawn the public criticism that they are simply too sensitive about sexual misconduct.

Kipnis's Case Against Sensitivity

I turn now to an illustrative example of contemporary criticism of Title IX and of sensitive students: the case—or perhaps, imbroglio—of Laura Kipnis, a professor in the School of Communication at Northwestern. Kipnis figures herself as a feminist scholar whose academic freedom to analyze Title IX has been threatened by sensitive students. In 2015, Kipnis published an article in the *Chronicle of Higher Education* entitled "Sexual Paranoia Strikes Academe." In it, Kipnis argues that university policies against sexual misconduct are causing students to think of themselves as "sensitive subjects": fragile, vulnerable, and unable to take a joke. Kipnis (2015a) writes, "Students were being encouraged to regard themselves as such exquisitely sensitive creatures that an errant classroom remark could impede their education, as such hothouse flowers that an unfunny joke was likely to create lasting trauma." Kipnis seems to imagine the academy as a place for students to learn to handle issues that may be challenging but ultimately can cause them no real harm. She asks, "But what do we expect will become of students, successfully cocooned from uncomfortable feelings, once they leave the sanctuary of academe for the boorish badlands of real life? What becomes of students so committed to their own vulnerability, conditioned to imagine they have no agency, and protected from unequal power arrangements in romantic life?" Kipnis argues that sensitive subjects ought to become *desensitized*, for their own good.

Kipnis's article goes on to describe details about two Title IX complaints filed against a philosophy professor at Northwestern by his students. She insinuates that the complainants are exaggerating, even lying, and litigious. After the article's publication, Kipnis *herself* became the subject of a Title IX investigation, since the policy also prohibits retaliation against complainants. Kipnis doubled down, publishing a follow-up article in the *Chronicle* entitled "My Title IX Inquisition," in which she describes reveling in the protests of student activists who objected to the article but being sobered (somewhat) by the investigation. In the second article, Kipnis construes herself and her fellow faculty as besieged: the publisher's illustration accompanying the article is an angry mob bearing megaphones and "I-X" pitchforks. Kipnis depicts the campus environment as a zero-sum game in which students are usurping the privileges of professors. Kipnis writes that "the more colleges devote themselves to creating 'safe spaces' . . . for students, the more dangerous those campuses become for professors. It's astounding how aggressive students' assertions of vulnerability have gotten in the past few years. Emotional discomfort is regarded as equivalent to material injury, and all injuries have to be remediated" (2015b). Kipnis seems to think that "emotional discomfort" is not a very serious thing to be at stake, and that claims of sexual harassment and assault, at least often ultimately, amount to only that, emotional discomfort. And that the vulnerability of students is also somehow making them into the aggressors. The aforementioned passage is quoted as evidence by other critics of students' sensitivity, such as the pseudonymous Edward Schlosser, who claimed in a 2015 *Vox* article to be so frightened of "consumerist" students' power that he had altered his curriculum.

Kipnis's second article also repeatedly invokes academic freedom as a value akin to the First Amendment's protection of free speech, although there is considerable debate among scholars, lawyers, and judges about both the reach and the foundation of academic freedom (as described in the introduction to this book). It's worth noting when scholars complain about students acting like consumers but appeal to the "marketplace of ideas" as a justification for academic freedom, as if the metaphor of an intellectual marketplace should only extend to those it figures as merchants, as if the responsibility for rhetorical engagement amounts to something like "buyer beware."

On the same day that the second article was published, Kipnis was found *not* responsible for retaliation, and she went on to publish a (nonacademic/non-peer-reviewed) book with Harper about both the philosophy professor's Title IX experience and her own (2017).[5] This was followed by yet another twist: the Title IX complainants who had filed against Kipnis for publishing identifying details about their cases in the *Chronicle* then sued Kipnis and Harper for publishing these and further private details in her book (apparently the suit was settled in November 2018). The book also prompted a group of graduate students in the Northwestern philosophy program to publish their own rebuttal to Kipnis's claims in the school newspaper. These students do not sound like hothouse flowers to me: They not only defend their colleague, one of the original complainants Kipnis wrote about, but they also answer Kipnis's assertion that academic freedom shields the kind of writing Kipnis was doing (and continued to do): they write, "We believe that there is a way to exercise academic freedom while still offering necessary protections to members of our community. This involves valuing not just academic freedom, but also privacy rights, intellectual integrity and professional standards" (Northwestern Philosophy Graduate Student Association 2017).

Kipnis paints herself as a misunderstood feminist martyr, especially in her contribution to a roundtable published in the feminist journal *Signs* about Kipnis's book ("Short Takes" 2017). But reactionary critics have taken Kipnis to be one of their own: a lawsuit filed against Secretary DeVos and the Department of Education, which alleged that DeVos's Title IX rules were developed based on discriminatory sexist animus, turned up an email from then deputy assistant secretary Candice Jackson, in which Jackson recommends Kipnis's book to her staff (Klein 2018). I doubt it was Kipnis's appeals to academic freedom that garnered Jackson's praise. Jackson had been instrumental in arranging meetings between men's rights groups and Department of Education staffers, including DeVos (see Barthélemy 2020). Kipnis's purportedly feminist critique of sensitive students was demonstrably recruited to support right-wing policy changes (see also the call at the end of Braceras 2017).

Sensitivity as a Critique of Sexual Power

I'm not saying academic freedom is unimportant; just the opposite: appeals to academic freedom are powerful appeals, and academic freedom is a crucial concept for scholars to study, articulate, and defend. But I don't agree that students are responsible for jeopardizing it when they advocate for or avail themselves of the Title IX process as a means of redressing the abuse of power in their universities. Following Sara Ahmed, I analyze public conversations about "problem students," like the one surrounding Kipnis, as a form of public debate over the university's norms and values. Criticizing students for failing to uphold these norms and values is also a way of calling for their reinforcement, and of missing what students themselves have to say about the harm university culture—and the circulation of sexual power within that culture—can do.

In a 2015 blog post entitled "Against Students," Ahmed traces how students are blamed for a range of ideological shifts in university culture, from "neoliberalism . . . [to] a new sexual puritanism." She notes that "the words 'moralism' and 'puritanism' are constantly being mobilised in anti-feminist writings"—and I point out, in feminist writings like Kipnis's, too—"because they allow a critique of power to be reframed (and dismissed) as an imposition of moral norms." I am not aiming to question Kipnis's sincerity, but to point out how the ideological context of her argument attaches it to, or articulates it with, interests that are inhospitable to the values she hopes to advance—like the freedom to critique the powerful.

Sexual harassment policy in the United States actually began with a critique of male power. Student activists today are directing that critique at unequal power relations that obtain not just between men and women, or even boss and employee, but also between teacher and student. Ahmed, who in 2016 resigned her professorship in protest of her university's failure to address the sexual harassment of students, writes in *Living a Feminist Life*: "Sexual harassment works . . . by increasing the costs of fighting against something, making it easier to accept something than to struggle against something, even if that acceptance is itself the site of your own diminishment; how you end up taking up less and less space" (2017, 141). In her blog, Ahmed urges us to take up a theoretical question that sensitive students have opened: "What does it mean to give or withhold consent . . . if the person asking for your consent holds power over you?"[6] In other words: What does it mean to be a sensitive subject, rather than a sovereign subject? This is a *rhetorical* question, one that joins sensitivity to questions of institutional power: What does it mean to be affected by another in conditions under which you are not able to decide whether you wish to permit this affection or to close it off?

That question is at the heart of this research. Recall Diane Davis's (2010) contention that our affectability as rhetorical existents is what gives language its powers to instantiate, as well as to move, or to wound. Rhetoricity makes symbolic action possible: it is the condition of possibility for being *able to respond* to symbols. But rhetoricity is not a simply optional relationship in which existents may choose to exercise their rhetorical power (or not). Rhetoricity itself depends on a prior rhetorical sensitivity that opens the rhetorical agent, subject, and existent to affection from outside. To be able to respond, we must first of all be sensitive, and this is my major claim—the sensitivity of rhetorical subjects is a generalized condition of possibility for rhetorical affection, and so for rhetorical relations.

When critics of sensitive students argue against sensitivity, they're often making a kind of layperson's claim about rhetorical theory: they advance a fantasy of a rhetorical subject for whom vulnerability and exposedness are simply matters of individual agentive choice—a valve you should just shut if you don't like what's coming your way. But if we look at sensitivity as a condition rather than a capacity, as an inability to stop oneself from being affected by an/other's address or affection, then what sensitivity names is a structural opening into the subject, one that also precedes the subject and makes it possible, through which rhetorical affection enters, not against our will but before it has even been constituted. And no matter how critics of sensitive students may bewail it, this rhetorical sensitivity can't simply be turned off or grown out of. The rhetorical relation we bear as rhetorical existents opens us, irreparably, one and all. "Sensitivity" can mark our fundamentally rhetorical exposedness. We are all sensitive subjects—students *and* professors alike. Every subject, to be what it is, is sensitive.

Sensitive Rhetoric, Institutional and Otherwise

Critiques of sensitivity like Kipnis's are commonplace in debates about Title IX, and they also have traction on a number of other issues that concern student activists. As rhetoricians trained to track the circulation of such arguments, and their imbrication with other submerged premises and ideological commitments, our job is to analyze and expose bad arguments, especially where they lead to bad policies. Title IX policies, as they are and were since at least 2011, have not been without their problems. Their most significant fault, in my view, is how the procedures of Title IX privilege the shielding of institutions from liability (and from the risk of losing federal funding, a punishment that has never yet been doled out). In her book on Title IX and institutional power, *Campus Sex, Campus Security,* Jennifer Doyle argues that "Title IX is the administrative structure through which the university knows what exposure feels like, what vulnerability *is*" (2015, 24). This is a fascinating claim; it suggests an *institutional* rhetoric of sensitivity in which the legal, financial, and perhaps ethical relations of the university are themselves structured by exposedness.[7] Insofar as Title IX policies are made to insulate the institution from any consequences of this exposedness, abuse of power will be covered up and ignored, and abusers sheltered, so long as their interests can be aligned with the institution's. The MacKinnonite faith in the power of the law to redress abuses of power in educational institutions may be necessary, but we can be sure it is not sufficient. In 2016, MacKinnon asked, "Why shouldn't schools be legally responsible in damages to students for violations of their sex equality rights—that is, for sexual harassment that meets substantive legal standards, meaning any failure to produce a learning environment that is sex-equal, free of sex-based abuse and violation? Why isn't the legal requirement, almost forty years after *Alexander v. Yale* was brought, that if sexual harassment is severe or pervasive or oppressive so as to make the learning environment unequal, schools are liable?" (2016, 2090). These questions can't simply be rhetorical.[8]

Yet the institutional rhetoric at work here may very well be part of what I am calling sensitive rhetorics. A rhetorical theory of sensitivity would affirm the exposedness of students, teachers, *and* institutions, and explore the differential ways that vulnerability is distributed through cultural beliefs and practices (and even material conditions). The repudiation of sensitivity by its critics has made it the center of public discussion about harm, feeling, and responsibility in the scene of the university. Making sensitivity the basis of a theory of rhetoric means engaging the term as the basis of a conversation about access to higher education, expert knowledge, and critical thought.

Sensitive rhetorics can help scholars understand the ideological as well as *affective* circuits that connect institutional power to everyday life. In their introduction to a special issue of the journal *Family Relations* entitled "Feminist Framings of Sexual Violence on College Campuses," Elizabeth Sharp and her coeditors write, "We were uncertain whether we had the emotional wherewithal to endure a sustained and heightened focus on sexual violence. . . . Many days we were unable to engage with the material" (2017, 8). This remark stands out to me because it marks the text with the affective labor that eventually *did* produce it, though not without energetic and emotional cost to the authors. We could think of this mark as tarnish on an otherwise polished text: it's a place where the work of scholarship *itself* is exposed as potentially disturbing. Writing about sexual violence is acknowledged here as draining; writing can be so draining that sometimes you can't write. How could this insight about scholarly sensitivity speak to and honor the experiences of our students? How could it enable us to better hear and respond to their requests for access to the academy that we now occupy? Sensitive rhetorics can help us take up these questions and develop answers that acknowledge the mutuality of our rhetorical exposedness, as well as the ethical responsibility that this exposedness institutes: to be a rhetorical subject, open to the affection of others, is to be a sensitive subject.

This chapter has shown how sensitivity structures debate about sexual harassment policies in higher education—namely, Title IX. Tied by its proponents to claims about academic freedom, critiques of sensitivity have won adherents not only among university and college faculty but among right-wing interests actively opposed to advancing the interests of women, students, and other minority groups. The sensitivity of students is amplified as a liability while the sensitivity of the institution is covered over. In the next chapter, I examine how sensitivity inflects the rhetoric of safe spaces through the lens of the wave of Black student activism in 2015–2016. Critiques of sensitivity sometimes include complaints that figure sensitive students as white, female, and overprivileged, yet Black student activists, as well as participants in the ensuing online conversation #BlackOnCampus, were targeted with many of the same critiques and accusations of oversensitivity. The next chapter looks at the issue of safe spaces through the lens of Black student activism after the occupation of the University of Missouri in late 2015. I contend that the occupation illustrates José Esteban Muñoz's framework of utopian performativity. The sensitivity of student activists gave them a way to both name *and* instantiate a safer future for Black students by and through the rhetoric of the demand.

Chapter 3

Racial (In)Sensitivity

Black Student Activism and the Demand for Safe Spaces

What do we owe each other for the sacrifices we each are called upon to make to rebuke and repair this world? How can we—those of us who profess to educate—accept the student demand not only as a rebuke, which it certainly is, but also as a gift?

Tav Nyong'o, "The Student Demand"

In chapter 2, I examined how critiques of sensitivity circulate in the debate over Title IX, specifically in its implementation as a sexual harassment policy in higher education. In this chapter, I study how critiques of sensitivity in the debate over safe spaces are inflected by racist premises and beliefs, even though (and because) race often goes unacknowledged in critiques of safe space activism. I center my analysis on the 2015 occupation of the University of Missouri's Carnahan Quad, and on the wave of occupations and student demands that followed it. In debates over trigger warnings and Title IX, the sensitive student is often uncritically imagined as an overprivileged middle-class white woman. Black students, though subject to trauma and sexual assault at higher rates than their peers (Edman, Watson, and Patron 2015; Frazier, Anders, and Perera 2009), are omitted from this predominant image. By examining contemporary Black student activism, I want to demonstrate how critiques of sensitivity manage to target a range of student activists beyond this narrow image, but do so by collapsing their diverse interests, tactics, and social positions into the image of the sensitive student. I argue that although race subtends contemporary debates over safe spaces, critiques of sensitivity function in this context to elide the demands of students of color. Yet Black students showed, through occupation and demand, that their sensitivity could have a performative power to transform the future.

In the fall of 2015, in response to a series of racist incidents on campus and inaction from university administrators, Black student activists using the name (and hashtag) #ConcernedStudent1950 (a reference to the year Black students were first admitted to the University of Missouri) organized a campout on the University of Missouri's Carnahan Quad. The occupation, which began on November 4, followed the announcement of a hunger strike by graduate student Jonathan Butler, demanding university president Tim Wolfe's resignation or removal. Shortly after the university's Black football players announced a strike in solidarity, Wolfe did resign and the occupation ended on November 9. After the occupation ended, students from Concerned Student 1950 continued to fuel a national conversation on race and higher education by asking Black students and alums to describe their experiences using the hashtag #BlackOnCampus. The day after the call, the BBC reported more than ninety thousand messages had been shared using the hashtag (Wendling 2015). At some campuses, students also organized fora on-site in which students, faculty, and staff could speak to the racial stress and conflict they face, especially at predominantly white institutions (PWIs). The widespread commonality of negative—and specifically, racist—experiences faced by students of color is also testified to in a growing body of literature on Black students' experiences of stigma and racism, as well as resistance and activism, in higher education research. Both online and off, #BlackOnCampus discussions evidence the specific experiences of *non*-safety—of vulnerability, threat, and harm—that Black members of campus communities frequently undergo.

After the occupation, student activists around the country also followed the example of Concerned Student 1950 and, joining a lengthy tradition of Black student activists in higher education, organized occupations of their own (Ahmad 1978; Biondi 2012; Kynard 2013; Rojas 2007). In some eighty instances, activists issued lists of demands, which were collected and published online at TheDemands.org.[1] Two separate scholarly analyses of this collection of demands found that they were primarily policy focused, calling for more resources for cultural centers and programming as well as increasing diversity among the faculty and student bodies (Chessman and Wayt 2016; Ndemanu 2017). In his analysis, Michael T. Ndemanu found that as many as two-thirds of demands included a request to create or support safe spaces on campus (2017, 242). These were specific and concrete requests: Ndemanu categorizes such calls alongside requests to fund Black cultural centers, to rename campus buildings or schools, and for universities to acknowledge both histories and recent incidents of harm (241). Despite the clarity of student demands for safe spaces, they are often treated by critics as if a "safe space" is a confusing and shifting ideological abstraction. In actuality, students have been quite clear and direct about the meaning of their requests for safe spaces.

I have chosen to focus this research on Black student activists in relation to safe spaces for two reasons. First, the University of Missouri occupation is an illustrative example of safe spaces activism, not only because it catalyzed similar activism around the country but also because activists declared the camp itself a safe space, and because this declaration was contested in a highly publicized way (which ended in the firing of a white assistant professor, Melissa Click—more on this later). Second, while Black students are not the only activists organizing occupations and demanding safe spaces (see, e.g., queer students discussed in Weida 2018 and Fox 2007, Native American students in Jackson 2017, or the Duke University Latinx student organization, Mi Gente 2016), they are in one sense the most visible: Mizzou was the eye of a storm of reporting and conversation about racism in higher education, even though several other campus occupations took place around the same time. But Black student activists are also displaced in criticism of sensitive students by a racist public imaginary that treats sensitivity as something like taste, a faculty of culture or refinement most (or only) available to white people (see Cottom 1981; Crowley 1995; Giroux 2000; Meyer 2000).

White people—yes, scholars, too—have a trained and ingrained tendency to overlook the way our whiteness insulates us from experiences of racial stress, displacing that stress onto people of color in our syllabi (DeChavez 2018), classrooms, faculty meetings, hiring processes (Sensoy and DiAngelo 2017), tenure and promotion proceedings (Carter and Craig 2022; Ward and Hall 2022), editorial review protocols (Stanley 2007), diversity committees (Ahmed 2012), elevators (Ore 2017), and otherwise everyday life on campus and off (Burrows 2020). I address this previous sentence specifically to other white scholars who may, like myself, tend to experience the university as a place where we are accorded respect, authority, and autonomy, by and large: such experience is frequently not accorded to our colleagues and students of color. In addition to offering an analysis of how the debate over sensitivity and safe spaces has helped sustain this white insulation, this chapter also represents a focused effort to exit my own racial comfort zone in order to offer a rhetorical critique of the debate over safe spaces that does not replicate its whiteness. Lisa Corrigan points out that "so little discourse among the larger community of rhetorical scholars addresses our role as stakeholders in the political health and social welfare of communities of color, both inside and outside of the academy, . . . even when the violence against them permeates university life" (2016, 86). Whiteness is insulating, which is to say whiteness provides, for those it privileges, a space predominantly free from racial stress—as well as from racial accountability.

It is in part this insulating quality of whiteness that makes some people think of whiteness as especially sensitive, as in cultivated, and that people of color are not as capable of this sort of feeling (see Cottom 1981; Giroux 2000; Meyer 2000; above). Ideologically, this premise works in tandem with its own opposite: that people of color (especially women of color) are excessively emotional, especially angry, such that any display of vulnerability can be criticized as inappropriate, irrational, and overly passionate (see Tomlinson 2010). But as I have argued in previous chapters, sensitivity is not a special capacity at all but a nonpower or passivity that exposes being to the affection of others in a rhetorical relation. This view raises questions about what "safe space" and "safety" can mean for students whose experiences of higher education are experiences of exclusion, precarity, and implicit as well as explicit threat. In this chapter, I aim to both pose and explore these questions, and to use them to shed light on what's at stake in the debate over safe spaces and its attendant critiques of sensitivity.

I begin this chapter by reviewing the context of events at the University of Missouri that shaped the 2015 occupation and its aftermath. I track the movement of media focus, which shifted away from the occupation and students' demands after a viral video showed a white faculty ally attempting to defend the activists' camp as a safe space. I then examine the way that beliefs about students' safety and possible exposure to harm and threat frame public debate about safe spaces. In examining how Black student activists have instantiated safe spaces at their institutions in and through their demands for safety, I argue that we should understand campus occupations like the one at Mizzou as worldmaking, a kind of utopian intervention in the realm of possibility that can change what arguments are hearable and available. I conclude by contending that rhetorical sensitivity poses a problem for the insulating power of whiteness. The worldmaking power of safe spaces depends on the prior nonpower of our rhetorical sensitivity.

The Occupation: Making and Defending a Safe Space

I turn first to an examination of the Mizzou occupation and the way that media coverage and public argument pivoted from the demands Black student activists had made (and won) to the critique of sensitivity targeting the demand for safe spaces. First, some further context for the Mizzou occupation. Recall that in 2015, public conversation about race and higher education was inflected by a video that surfaced that spring at the University of Oklahoma of the Sigma Alpha Epsilon fraternity members singing a racist chant (Berrett 2015). In October, Yale students hotly engaged instructors and residential leaders who questioned an Intercultural Affairs Council message asking students to rethink potentially offensive Halloween costumes (S. Brown 2015). In December, the Supreme Court would hear oral arguments in *Fisher vs. The University of Texas*, in which a white woman who did not qualify for admission to the University of Texas at Austin sued over the use of race in university admissions. It was two and a half years after the murder of Trayvon Martin; a year after the murder of Michael Brown.[2] It was June 2015 that a white supremacist shooter had murdered nine people at a Bible study at Emanuel African Methodist Episcopal Church in Charleston, South Carolina.

Jonathan A. McElderry and Stephanie Hernandez Rivera were both mid-level administrators working in campus cultural centers at the University of Missouri during the events of late 2015. I draw on their excellent summary of the immediate history, context, and events at Mizzou, which begins one year prior with the murder of Michael Brown in Ferguson, Missouri, in August 2014.[3] According to McElderry and Rivera, "three queer Black women began organizing their peers" before the fall 2014 semester began with a "Hands Up, Don't Shoot" photo campaign (2017, 319). I want to underline that it was queer Black women who, as in other revolutionary spaces, laid this groundwork. In the fall, a multiracial student coalition reached out to administrators, requesting a meeting to present a list of demands they had titled "Calls to Action" (319). In the spring of 2015, students were frustrated with "the administration's lack of transparency and accountability," but by the fall of 2015, many student organizers of these efforts had graduated (319)—student turnover often works in administrations' favor. A *New York Times* article from November 10 notes that graduate students began organizing before the semester started when the university told them it would no longer contribute to their health insurance costs (Pérez-Peña and Hauser 2015). Although the university reversed the decision, the grad students had begun working on unionization, and allied with campus antiracism activists. I also want to underline that the coalition of antiracist organizers and grad student labor organizers was also foundational to what followed.

In the fall of 2015, McElderry and Rivera write, students met continuing racist incidents on campus with mobilization, culminating in a demonstration at homecoming in October that "halted the annual homecoming parade to address the university system President Tim Wolfe about his lack of acknowledgement and response to racial incidents on campus" (2017, 319–20). Black students, backs turned, blocked the parade route in front of Wolfe's car. As if to exemplify disregard for the students' interests, demands, and even physical safety, Wolfe "tapped" a protestor with his car when he tried to maneuver around the students (Pearson 2015). Under the name Concerned Student 1950, Black student activists issued a new list of demands. In addition to calling for the removal of President Wolfe, they called on the university to meet demands first issued by the Legion of Black Collegians in 1969. They demanded a "racial awareness and inclusion curriculum," an increase in the percentage of Black faculty and staff to 10%, a strategic plan for retaining Black students, and material support for campus mental health resources and social justice centers (Concerned Student 1950, 2015). In late October, while activists waited for a response from administrators, someone drew a swastika on a residence hall wall using feces (Pearson 2015). Administrators met with members of Concerned Student 1950 but wouldn't accede to their demands. By November 3, graduate student Jonathan Butler announced a hunger strike demanding Tim Wolfe's resignation or removal. McElderry and Rivera note "that none of this student's friends or peers knew he would be embarking on this hunger strike. He announced it to the fellow members of #Concerned-Student1950 the day before he e-mailed the system president, Board of Curators, and blind-copied various in[di]viduals, including us" (2017, 320).[4]

The hunger strike was an accelerant: it spurred the campout on the Carnahan Quad in solidarity with Butler, who also met with Black members of the football team. The day after the meeting, the team, supported by the head coach (see Kelderman 2015), announced a strike that would have cost the university "upwards of five million dollars" (McElderry and Rivera 2017, 320). The protestors had a found a way to touch the university's financial nerve, and in so doing garnered the attention of the national news media. The institution's sensitivity to a financial threat was a powerful lever. McElderry and Rivera write, "On Monday, November 9, after nearly seven days of the student's hunger strike, and less than 48 hours after the football team announced they would refuse to play, Tim Wolfe resigned" (2017, 320). They also note that the joy of student activists was tempered by a wave of backlash, which included "death threats against the protestors, Black students on campus, and harm done to the Black Culture Center,"[5] as well as threats to state funding from Missouri legislators, a significant drop in university-wide enrollment, and a "mass exodus of faculty and staff" (320). Moreover, headlines about the student activists' success gave way to a media focus on a "safe spaces" controversy sparked by the actions of a white faculty member who supported the students on the quad.

On the morning of November 9, as news of Wolfe's resignation reached the camp, protestors put up signs declaring the camp a safe space and specifically asking the media to keep their distance (Bates 2015). Only the night before, someone displaying a Confederate flag had driven a truck around the campus, an apparent attempt to intimidate protestors. Allies at the camp that morning, including communication professor Melissa Click, formed a human ring around the camp to shield the organizers and allow them time to strategize about their response to the resignation. Two students approached the ring: Tim Tai, a student journalist on freelance assignment for ESPN, not wearing any credentials; the other, Mark Schiebecker, not on assignment, taping the interaction between Tai and the protestors. After several tense minutes, Tai is rebuffed, but Schiebecker advances, walking up to Click and asking, "I'm media, can I talk to you?" Click tells him several times to get out. Schiebecker's video of the exchange, in which Click calls out, "Who wants to help me get this reporter out of here? I need some muscle over here," went viral. Although Click apologized the next day, both publicly and then personally to the students, a social media campaign began under the hashtag #FireMelissaClick, sustaining pressure on the school administration—and ultimately providing cover for their eventual decision to fire Click in February (Stein, Barton, and Paul 2017). The decision was made by the University of Missouri system's Board of Curators.

Click's case became an important moment that ties student activism to academic freedom, as well as a potential site of a fracture in student/faculty solidarity. The American Association of University Professors issued an investigative report condemning Click's firing, as well as the Board's denial of Click's request for a hearing before a duly constituted faculty body. The AAUP report also found that the calls for Click's firing made by members of the Missouri legislature exerted undue political influence on Click's case. The university system did what was in its own interest as a financial and political entity, not what would have been procedurally fair or academically rigorous. Click's case illustrates how free speech concerns—including both academic freedom and freedom of the press—can converge in ways that occlude the issues and activists that occasioned their exercise. Click (a faculty member, a white woman) became the big story, displacing Wolfe's resignation and the successful pressure exerted by Black student activists.

Click's case also illustrates how overt racial conflicts like those at Mizzou were buried, even as they continue to animate the contemporaneous conversation about safe spaces.[6] The disappearance of race from the larger public conversation about safe spaces can be traced in the hard turn taken by media coverage of the Mizzou occupation away from the success of student activists and toward the supposed threat their request for safe spaces posed to free speech and the free press. As a result, the centrality of race to the contemporary conversation about safe spaces has been eclipsed by critiques of sensitivity. Although Wolfe had resigned, it was Click's actions that dominated headlines about Mizzou. The next day, the *Atlantic* published an op-ed with the headline "Campus Activists Weaponize 'Safe Space.'" Although the piece acknowledges that activists' main concern was racism on campus, and that protestors had been explicit with signs and on social media about requesting privacy from the press, the author accuses the activists of "twisting the concept of 'safe space'" (Friedersdorf 2015). The bulk of the piece is a description of the Click viral video, and the tone is one of incredulity that activists would view the persistent approach of even an uncredentialed student journalist as an incursion on space they were occupying. Roderick A. Ferguson argues that demeaning student movements is a systemic strategy "used by and on behalf of dominant institutions to discredit the kinds of connections that can lead to social transformation" (2017, 68). Critiques like Friedersdorf's amplified the topoi of safe spaces, making it appear to casual readers that the "weapon" of safe spaces dominated the scope of activists' concerns—making it appear that students' top priority was their own sensitivity.

Another op-ed at the *Los Angeles Times* took a similar tack, focusing on Click's actions and amplifying the point of view widely held by journalists, describing the activists as "commandeering a public square and hassling journalists who are trying to record a public protest" (McGough 2015). An NPR report (with the tongue-in-cheek title "Hands Up Don't Shoot: Thoughts from the Mizzou Photog Blocked during Protest"—the main title phrase a double reference to Ferguson protestors' chant after the murder of Michael Brown and, gratingly, to the Mizzou protestors' hands blocking the photographer's camera shot; Bates 2015) enumerates several important questions of journalistic ethics raised by the incident: "how the media covers communities of color; whether having the legal right to document an event is balanced by a moral right to carefully and respectfully approach communities that are often marginalized and misreported on; and whether one should continue to take photos if the subjects of the story adamantly object"—but gives voice not to the protestors but to Tai (who was quite gracious about the incident in his many interviews). Even when the specific and complex stakes of the issue are acknowledged and named, the perspective of the outsider journalist is centered and naturalized as objective.

Some scholars worked to recontextualize the incident. In their statement of support for Melissa Click and Concerned Student 1950, a group of feminist and critical media scholars write: "We find that Click's taped actions, in fact, demonstrate support for students who felt unsafe in the face of violent threats issued against them on their university campus—both by protestors in the public Mizzou spaces and residence halls, and via social media ... viral video footage fails as evidence because it shows only one part of a larger story. ... Feminist media scholars understand that the individual holding the camera, rather than the subject of the camera, is deemed to hold greater power" (Wu 2016). The statement also underscores that "there was significant campus unrest and no security was present to ensure safety" (Wu 2016) in the immediate aftermath of Wolfe's resignation. The campout on the Carnahan Quad was never safe: student activists exposed themselves to the intervention of campus security[7] and local police, to say nothing of the observation of news media and the pointedly addressed intimidation performed by other members of the campus and local communities. When Click tried to intervene to protect the students assembled on the morning of November 9, her goal was to honor their request for time and privacy to process the change they had just effected, and to deliberate together about how to respond to and represent it. One of these activists had been on a hunger strike for nearly seven days. They knew they had a national spotlight on their actions, one at least the size and brightness of college football. Click was defending the space that students had not only requested but *created* to begin with through the act of occupation.

In *Cruising Utopia: The Then and There of Queer Futurity* (2009), José Esteban Muñoz argues that utopian desiring is both a route of access to a queer future and a performative way of calling this future into the realm of the possible. The campout on the Carnahan Quad ought to be viewed as a paradigmatic example of student activists seeking—and creating—a safe space precisely because the students at Mizzou instantiated this very space in their occupation. They put themselves at substantial risk, but they drew on overlapping networks of solidarity to secure one another's well-being—networks that included undergrad and grad students, queer students, multiracial students, grad student labor organizers, and untenured and otherwise vulnerable members of the faculty. Acting out of their sensitivity was both a utopian action and an instantiating one. The action of occupation not only effected Wolfe's resignation but, moreover, the occupation and the students' demands performatively opened a possible world that other students around the country pursued by organizing semipublic fora about their experiences as Black students with the hashtag #BlackOnCampus, and by issuing demands of their own.

Safety, Harm, and Threat

While researching this chapter, I was struck by the similarities between experiences of harm and threat described in the #BlackOnCampus conversation and experiences documented by scholars studying Black students in higher education, such as those recounted to Joe R. Feagin and Melvin P. Sikes and described in their 1995 article "How Black Students Cope with Racism on White Campuses." Black students were and are weary of white students telling racist jokes, or assuming that Black students must be athletes, or are otherwise the beneficiaries of unmerited affirmative action. Other forms of common and subtle discrimination (sometimes called microaggressions, see Solorzano, Ceja, and Yosso 2000) include overemphasizing the success of Black students, as if they are exceptional among peers of their race; unfair treatment from professors and other authorities, including biased responses to discussion of racial issues; cultural bias, such as ignorance of the intense emotion that can accompany discussion of histories (or current events) in which Black people are violently subjugated (Feagin and Sikes 1995, 95); and the labeling of Black support groups as separatist, militant, or simply a minority interest (i.e., not beneficial to the whole campus).

Contemporary research on Black students' experience in higher education demonstrates more of the same. Writing in 2017, Seanna Leath and Tabbye Chavous argue the marginalization of Black students at PWIs "undermine[s] their sense of belonging" (2017, 221), and that Black students' experience of stigma in their first year at PWIs changed their beliefs about societal equity and fairness (233). Bryan K. Hotchkins and T. Elon Dancy (2017) contend that a hostile residential campus climate can impact Black students' academic outcomes. Veronica A. Jones and Richard J. Reddick (2017) demonstrate that while many students choose to engage in campus activism because of negative experiences, this engagement has a cost: the time and emotions students invest in activism amounts to a tax on their well-being. Ginnie Logan, Brian A.

Lightfoot, and Ana Contreras (2017) found that for some student activists, making a safe space within a hostile campus context became more important after the 2016 election in response to the intensification of racial conflict and stress (258). Despite many universities' rhetoric of diversity—and its use as a marketing asset—on many campuses inclusion is still tokenized and its transformative potential curtailed (see Ahmed 2012).

Understanding students' request for safe spaces on their campuses requires scholars to understand the context of harm and threat in which students articulate their demands for safety. In part because of its high media profile, the Mizzou occupation was viewed as a model for other Black student activists around the country. The #BlackOnCampus conversation helped students at different campuses come to identify their experiences with those of the activists at Mizzou, as Bryan K. Hotchkins notes in his study of Black student leaders at PWIs (2017, 274). Hotchkins finds that student leaders sought "to locate exclusive Black spaces where solidarity and strategy occurred" in order to organize for change at their schools (278). Strategies that Hotchkins terms "racial resistance" helped students "to avert race-based trauma" (270) through a process of racial socialization. This cultural knowledge gave Hotchkins's participants a sense of responsibility for "building and sustaining Black college communities" (273–74). Student activists found that they must organize to sustain one another: having a safe space preceded and made possible any other kind of activism for students at predominantly white institutions.

The need that precipitated the #BlackOnCampus hashtag was that the experiences of Black students are often not visible to non-Black stakeholders because of a dynamic Diane Lynn Gusa has identified as "White institutional presence." In a 2010 article in the *Harvard Educational Review*, Gusa uses White institutional presence to name "the racialized influences on discourses between and among students, between student[s] and teachers, and between students and academic resources" (467). Crucial to Gusa's concept is a view of whiteness as "not only a cultural location but a sociological and political construct of power that allows Whites to assert superiority over those who are not White" (468). White institutional presence consists of four "intricately linked attributes":

1. White ascendancy, which refers to control over racial discourse and a sense of entitlement to do so;
2. monoculturalism, in which White structures of knowledge, professionalism, and scholarship are accorded the highest status;
3. White blindness, which is the belief that race is immaterial and/or irrelevant; and
4. White estrangement, which is the failure of White people to associate interracially, even out of insecurity or ignorance. (472)

The concept of White institutional presence can help non-Black stakeholders understand the context students of color must frequently navigate at predominantly white institutions of higher education: isolation from peers, devaluation by instructors and administrators, and discouragement from participating in campus life—all couched in the denial that any of it is happening.

White institutional presence can be understood as a cause of repetitive and persistent injuries for students of color. Feagin and Sikes describe the all-permeating effect of White institutional presence in schools: "When black students say 'whiteness' is an omnipresent problem, they are not just talking about color or racial identification. They are reporting being at sea in a hostile environment. Painful difficulties with teachers, fellow students, and curricula not only accumulate year after year for black children as individuals and as a group but also regularly bring to mind the collective memory of past discrimination" (1995, 97). What does a safe space for Black students look like in this context? What does *safety* look like, or feel like? Feagin and Sikes argue that the failure of white institutions to truly desegregate—"to incorporate black values, interests, or history into the core of campus culture"—encourages Black students "to congregate in their own groups and plan their own activities" (91), a self-protective response viewed by white institutions as self-segregation. Yet the relative safety of being with people who are more likely to share your experiences is repeatedly described in the literature, drawn from Black students' experience, as crucial to both survival and success in PWIs.

Some critics of sensitive students did seem to take note of the relation between sensitivity and race in campus issues, even in advance of the occupation of Mizzou. In March 2015, the *New York Times* published an op-ed entitled "In College and Hiding From Scary Ideas." In it, contributing op-ed writer Judith Shulevitz criticizes the concept of safe spaces, calling them "the live-action version of the better-known trigger warning." Linking safe spaces to trigger warnings is a rhetorical move that allows critics to invoke arguments against students' sensitivity, and it's a move that's fairly common in popular critiques of safe spaces (see, e.g., Ellison cited in Jaschik 2016; Shapiro 2014; and others cited in Weida 2018). Shulevitz's piece is worth mentioning here because it clearly racializes the critique of sensitivity. Shulevitz gives two histories of the safe space: the first she draws from second-wave feminist consciousness-raising meetings, blaming feminists for what critics see as more generalized problems with contemporary student culture.[8] But Shulevitz also indicts critical race theory, name-checking legal scholar Mari J. Matsuda for propagating the idea that "the First Amendment should not safeguard language that inflict[s] emotional injury through racist or sexist stigmatization." The claim attributed to critical race theorists is that language can do harm, and that symbolic violence is still violence, and so it ought to be distinguished from constitutionally protected free speech.[9]

Despite Shulevitz's attack on critical race theory, the article is accompanied by an illustrated image of a white woman curled into the fetal position inside of an ear, at once invoking and recirculating the image of the oversensitive student as infantile, feminine, and white. Yet more than once, the article insinuates or overtly contends that it's not students but faculty or even guest speakers who are under threat from such students, and "in need of a safer space." Shulevitz's criticism exemplifies the view that oversensitive students are simply too coddled, too insulated, and even "self-infantilizing" when they seek to create safe spaces on their campuses. The harm and threat of being #BlackOnCampus is erased in order to make the claim that language can cause harm appear to be hyperbolic and irrational. The need for safety disappears if those people who are asking for safety are disparaged as coddled and actually *themselves* threatening to others. Understanding the constellations of safety, harm, and threat at work in critiques of safe spaces is necessary context for understanding the exigence and effectivity of the activist interventions being criticized.

Yet the framework of safety, harm, and threat is complicated by the social and institutional roles occupied by universities and the individuals within them. In *Writing against Racial Injury* (2015), one of the few publications on contemporary student activism in composition studies, Haivan V. Hoang argues that the rhetoric of "racial injury" deals out limited roles from which individuals can speak about racial issues: the available roles position speakers as either victim, aggressor, or savior. Drawing on ethnographic observation of a Vietnamese American student coalition, Hoang shows how liberal discourses of diversity and multiculturalism limit the arguments available to students of color and ultimately damage their pursuit of racial justice. Hoang's critique of the rhetorical constraints of racial injury can help us understand the context to which students of color are responding in the debate over safe spaces. While critics claim that student activists are confining themselves to the role of victims, they miss the larger rhetorical dynamic in which students' arguments are framed as "victimology," and the concomitant positioning of the critic as either aggressor or savior. By examining the Mizzou occupation as a specific example of Black student activists organizing a safe space, I aim to show how the demand for and instantiation of safe spaces on campus can exceed the framework of racial injury. Declaring the campout on the Carnahan Quad to be a safe space, even in the midst of intense conflict and media attention, can be understood as both a concrete strategy for self-protection and a utopian act of worldmaking.

Safe Spaces as Worldmaking

Outside of the contemporary debate over safe spaces in which they are aligned with trigger warnings as a sign of students' oversensitivity, some scholars have criticized safe space campaigns for their failure to challenge structural inequities. Catherine Fox argues in a 2007 article that LGBT "safe space" and "ally" sticker campaigns "create a safe space for folks to feel free from the guilt of homophobia and heterosexism" without actually confronting their complicity with white heteronormativity (503). Fox questions, "What if queers were to *demand* safe space? How might this demand change the power relations between those who 'create' safe spaces and those who are intended to benefit from such spaces?" (503). This query focuses our attention on the rhetorical effectivity of the demand;[10] it suggests that the act of demanding safe space is an intervention in the balance of power between those who are not safe and those who already have safety—and who can work to "create" it for others. Roderick A. Ferguson has called the demand "the initial utterance of insurgency," contending that the demand can work "to elevate the crises happening in communities that would otherwise go unheard to the level of the social, making those crises public and worthy of an organized response" (2017, 6). Student activists at Mizzou in 2015 exercised the language of the demand, but they also declared their occupation a safe space (Logue 2015)—an enactment of the future they demanded.

If we apply Muñoz's utopian framework, students' safe spaces can be understood as activist enactments of a rhetorical futurity that, as I've argued elsewhere, makes arguments that are circulating in one community more readily available to rhetors in other conversations: "When the available means are insufficient, we have to make more arguments available; we have to widen the scope of the possible. Our politics become utopian: we have to look beyond what is given, to another possible world" (Gerdes 2019a, 233). Demands are made when negotiation is not possible, when leaders and administrators have been closed to students' voices for so long that the claims and requests of those voices, going unheard, become unhearable. Intractable circumstances—impasse—call for both the creativity to maneuver "inside or around an impasse" and a kind of defiant hope that impasse can and will ultimately give way (Cvetkovich 2012, 21). When student activists are told or shown that change is not possible, answering with utopianism can be a transformative response.

The Mizzou students' occupation—and their concomitant declaration of safe space on a decidedly unsafe campus—was an act of utopianism because it defies what Muñoz called "the prison house" of "the here and now" (2009, 1) in favor of calling an otherwise unavailable future into the realm of possibility. Rhetoricians will recognize this sort of action as the work of rhetorical invention: of making more arguments available. I have argued, following Muñoz, that such interventions are performatives,[11] attempts "to instantiate a future, to call it from potentiality into actuality, to beckon it with not only words and not only actions but even with dreams and feelings" (Gerdes 2019a, 237). The declaration of a safe space, accompanied by the demand for policies to make the rest of the space of the university safer, creates a productive performative contradiction: the occupation becomes an *enactment* of the very future that's demanded, joining the here and now to a then and there by both anticipating that future and instantiating it. Students' sensitivity became the basis for their utopian intervention.

The success, or—to draw on the vocabulary promulgated by speech act theorist J. L. Austin (1962)—the felicity of the performative does not simply depend on achieving the goals that students intended. The achievement of the occupation can't be measured by the university's response to students' demands alone. Effecting the president's resignation, for example, alters the conditions on which the students' other demands can potentially be heard—and not only at the University of Missouri. One 2016 study of administrative response to student demands found that 75% of presidents at four-year institutions said recent events had increased the racial dialogue at their schools. The survey of more than 560 college presidents found that "as a result of student activism, [their schools] are working on the following actions: implementing cultural competency training (19 percent), developing or revising curriculum (19 percent), increasing diversity (9 percent) and allocating resources for support services for students of color (8 percent)" (Espinosa, Chessman, and Wayt 2016; see also Rankin 2016).[12] Notably, presidents of four-year schools reported a higher level of responsiveness to racial justice activism than two-year schools; public institutions were also more likely than private schools to take action.

A number of studies have found that the administrative response to Black student activism reflects a concern for universities' public image rather than a commitment to students of color (Bradley 2017; see also Schmidt 2015), reflecting a neoliberal order of priorities. Rema Reynolds and Darquillius Mayweather point out that the threat of a public relations embarrassment can be motivating for institutions; yet, they contend, the isolated victories yielded through such convergence of interests won't "yield [the] exponential effects needed for systemic, institutional change in policy and practice" (2017, 299). Student activism is difficult to sustain; administrations have the advantage of mostly staying put while student populations turn over every few years. This is one of the reasons transformational change is so hard to effect in higher education: students' momentum suffers when they have to constantly reinvent their activist communities. But even incremental changes do have one powerful rhetorical quality to recommend them: they can change what arguments are available.

And yet, this is as true of progressive changes as it is of regressive ones: after the 2016 election, white supremacist action spiked around the country, including on college campuses. In February 2017, the Southern Poverty Law Center documented 1,372 reported bias incidents since the election, with more than 65 incidents of hate flyers posted on campuses, advertising such white supremacist slogans as "Imagine a Muslim-Free America" (Hatewatch 2017; Jaschik 2017; L. Ellis 2017). Universities tended to respond to these postings in a bizarrely procedural fashion: at UT Austin, for example, spokesperson J. B. Bird stated, "The university vigorously supports free speech, but posting signs of any nature on the outside of university buildings is not allowed under campus rules" (L. Ellis 2017). Such statements imply that the posters *could* constitute free speech and *might* be allowed, if they had only been posted in accordance with the university's policy. The university's message fails to affirm that Muslim students belong at the school, and that diversity of backgrounds, beliefs, and religion enriches the learning community. Instead, the university communicates their vigorous support *for seeking permission* to post signs advocating for the elimination of Muslim Americans, specifically on the inside and not the outside of university buildings. In the push-and-pull of contest over what kinds of speech are accepted as defensible as well as normal or commonplace on college campuses, ground can be gained or lost in the way that institutions choose to respond to instances of hate speech and threats of violence, tacit and otherwise.

The performative success of the occupation, and of the declaration of a safe space in the midst of exposure to great risk, is itself made possible by student activists' embrace of their own sensitivity, despite critics' opposition of sensitivity to free speech and academic freedom. In an article published in the *AAUP Journal of Academic Freedom*, Jaime Weida (2018) argues that safe spaces should be understood as a way of protecting free speech, and that advocates of including hate speech under the umbrella of free speech are making a specious argument. Weida points out the double standard such advocates apply: "Hate speech is defended as free speech, and discourse addressing hate speech is dismissed as censorship" (5). Weida points out that harassment undermines students' ability to learn, and she rightly contends that if schools allow their students to be harassed, then students will understand their schools are endorsing the harassment (which, by the way, is the theory of harassment law that governs the university's financial liabilities under Title IX—see chapter 2). The sensitivity of Black students to the repetitive stress injury that is white institutional presence is what causes student activists to demand safe spaces on campus. The insensitivity of critics to the harms of white institutional presence is, simply put, a function of insulating privilege.

Let me note here that if students are demanding and making safe space for themselves on campus, it is because safe space has *not* been provided to them by their institutions. This is a failure for which faculty and administrators together bear responsibility. Journalists and op-ed writers weren't the only ones to attack student demands for safe spaces. At the start of the academic year following the occupation of Mizzou, a highly publicized letter to incoming students from a dean at the University of Chicago framed safe spaces as a "retreat from ideas and perspectives at odds with [one's] own" (Ellison quoted in Jaschik 2016). In a law review article on student protests, Philip Lee points out that the dean's letter "fail[s] to consider the academic freedom of the student protestors" (2018, 267), whose actions also articulated controversial ideas and perspectives. Weida's analysis demonstrates how administrative opposition to safe spaces actually impinges on the academic freedom of instructors "to designate their classrooms or other educational spaces 'safe' if they wish to do so for legitimate pedagogical reasons" (2018, 11–12). She notes that "classroom safe spaces are especially important for classes that deal with nondominant ideologies and identities," because students need to feel safe to challenge hegemonic beliefs (6)—and to share ideas and perspectives that might be at odds with those of their instructors and peers.

To put this issue in rhetorical terms, we are talking about the right to speak, as well as what resources it actually takes for students to exercise that right on campus. Political theorist Teresa M. Bejan (2017) frames this in terms of the ancient Greek concepts of *isegoria* and *parrhesia*, drawing a distinction between the license to say whatever you want (*parrhesia*) and the right to equal democratic participation (*isegoria*). By attacking students' sensitivity, critics of safe spaces shift the terms of the debate away from this issue of equal rhetorical agency, actually central to the exercise of free speech, and away from the ordinary violence one is exposed to simply by being Black on campus. In an open letter that preceded the Mizzou occupation by a few weeks, a group of "concerned and unapologetic" students of color at Wesleyan University point out that their speech is not construed as the exercise of free speech. In white institutions, Black students are not viewed as rhetorical subjects, so their speech is not heard as speech that must be protected. The Wesleyan students write:

> When students of color speak our lives into existence, our speech comes under attack. When we defend our lives, we are harassing you. When we demand safety, we are attacking you. Our unapologetic voices are deranged screams; our open hands are clenched fists; our cellphones, weapons, our pigment, targets. Centering this conversation on free speech, without the context of the voices historically censored and misrepresented, is the very manifestation of systemic and structural racism that continues to silence and murder people of color. (A Group of Concerned and Unapologetic Students of Color 2015, quoted in Lee 2018, 267)

If the opposite of retreating from ideas and perspectives that differ from one's own is engaging them—if that is what we want our students to do—then we have to account for the unequal ways that engagement is defined, perceived, and rewarded, especially in predominantly white institutions of higher education.

Safe Spaces in Pedagogy

So let's take a closer look now at the connection between safe spaces that students instantiate and safe spaces in the classroom. The concept of the campus or classroom as a safe space predates current critiques of sensitive students by at least a decade (more if you connect it to second-wave feminist consciousness-raising; see Evans 1979). In a 2005 article, Lynn C. Holley and Sue Steiner draw on a tradition of research on safe spaces in the social work classroom dating to 1998. Holley and Steiner sought to compare the views of students on safe spaces to those of instructors: they smartly argue that "without this information, instructors may create classroom environments that they believe support honest dialogue and participation, but from students' perspectives, actually do not" (2005, 49–50). Noting that in a curriculum full of difficult issues—and in classrooms full of diverse students—"it may be unrealistic to expect any classroom to be truly safe for all students" (62), Holley and Steiner contend that instructors should strive to create a *safer* space. They also note that "for students of color, inclusion of cultural content is important in the creation of safe space" (60)—that is, for students who are racially marked, addressing race and its impact on the disciplinary issues under study is a crucial part of what it means for a classroom to be safe(r). Students in this context are by no means shying away from hard conversations.

Yet for teachers of rhetoric and perhaps writing in particular, the relationship between conflict, trauma, and what we and our students do in our classrooms is a fraught one. Peter N. Goggin and Maureen Daly Goggin, in their contribution to the collection *Trauma and the Teaching of Writing*, argue that it's crucial for writing teachers "to recognize that the classroom is *not* a safe place" (2005, 39). They point out that the classroom is "not hermetically sealed off from the world in which it is situated" (39). Not only students' but instructors' histories with racial privilege, discrimination, and violence enter our classrooms with each of us. Goggin and Goggin contend that studying "the interdependent relation between trauma and writing" can itself "illuminate the shadowy aspects of safety and community that are often (and naively) presumed in the writing class" (39). Trauma is not only a single disruptive event; trauma is often the prolonged daily experience of insecurity, of being mistrusted, misrepresented, and misunderstood.

Scholars and teachers of rhetoric and composition have long believed that fostering vigorous and responsible arguments is a core part of our work. Susan Jarratt, in "Feminism and Composition: The Case for Conflict," answers the feminist canards that argument and authority are inherently violent—or at least, more violent than the vacuum created in their absence from the composition classroom. Jarratt points out that the structures of power of the dominant culture are reproduced in the classroom such that no group of writers could truly be "value-free." With an eye toward the history of rhetoric, Jarratt advocates that feminist composition should treat "the inevitability of conflict" as a "starting point . . . through which the inequalities generating those conflicts can be acknowledged and transformed" (1991, 119). But to refract this analysis through the experience of students of color can help us see what's at stake when we ask, encourage, or fail to adequately prepare for our students to engage in conflicts over racial inequalities in higher education, within our classrooms and without.

Racial (In)Sensitivity and White Insulation

White institutional presence already furnishes safety to those critics, scholars, and students accredited by their whiteness. Weida points out that demands for safe spaces are necessarily minoritarian, because minority voices are drowned out by an imbalance of power: "Currently, the United States is 'safe' primarily for privileged, cisgender, white (predominantly male) voices and bodies. These voices do not need additional safe spaces for their narratives and identities. The world is their safe space" (2018, 6). Critiques of safe spaces that deny the legitimacy of students' sensitivity are denying the rhetorical relation on which effective rhetorical engagement depends. Whiteness works by denying the sensitivity of its others, and by denying its own sensitivity *to* these others. Yet denying this sensitivity does not destroy it. As whiteness insulates itself and its members from feeling their exposedness to others, it amplifies its own violence while simultaneously drowning it out. Attacking the sensitivity of student activists who are demanding safe spaces may change the ground of the argument, but it won't erase the need for safety and belonging that this student demand articulates.

As Concerned Student 1950 demonstrated, the occupation and the demand have to come from a place of sensitivity. If students could shield themselves from this rhetorical violence, if they weren't sensitive, there would be no need for the demand, no impetus for the occupation. Some critics argued that asking the institution to redress students' grievances would never be sufficient. Such criticism misses how the act of occupation—organizing as a community and as a coalition, showing solidarity across campuses, physically asserting the right to be here and to be respected and yes, even protected the way that white students are protected—is also a performative act, an intervention in the conditions of the moment and in the conditions of the possible. Understood as an act of utopianism, the occupation enacts the future it seeks, rupturing the stultifying constraints of the here and now. Like any performative, its results may be otherwise than intended, but even in the *attempt* to call a better future into being, student activists reveal the rhetorical work that being together, feeling together, and dreaming together can accomplish.

This chapter has shown how sensitivity inflects the rhetoric of safe spaces through the lens of Black student activism. Although the sensitive student is often figured as an overprivileged white woman, critiques of safe spaces invoked this image in ways that elide the diverse race, gender, and class backgrounds of student activists. Examining the 2015 occupation at the University of Missouri, and the way that media attention shifted the day of the president's resignation from the student activists' success to the propriety of a white faculty ally's actions, reveals how the concern for academic freedom and free speech can be instrumentalized by critics of sensitive students. Critiques of sensitivity can be used to overshadow the harm and threat that students of color are exposed to in predominantly white institutions, and with them the centrality of race to demands for safe spaces. The hashtag #BlackOnCampus and the student demands issued in its wake show how deliberation in a semipublic space can and does work rhetorically to effect institutional (if incremental) change. A safe space to be sensitive—to reflect, to feel, and to deliberate with one's community—that's a precondition for surviving in institutions never meant to welcome you. The utopianism of staying sensitive insists on a more just future. The next chapter turns to focus on predominantly white student organizing in the debate over campus carry laws. Campus carry is unique as a contemporary issue in student activism because claims about free speech and academic freedom are aligned *with* the party construed as sensitive, rather than against them. By historicizing the debate over campus carry in Texas, the next chapter shows that critiques of sensitivity will cut loose from free speech and academic freedom if those values oppose critics' stronger ideological commitments.

Chapter 4

Vulnerability to Violence

An Account of Campus Carry in Texas

Neither "total annihilation" nor murder by figuration delivers me from my exposedness to radical alterity, from my vulnerability, affectability, susceptibility to an absolutely inappropriable exteriority—nor, therefore, does it deliver me from my obligation, my responsibility to respond, which precedes and makes possible any idea of freedom.

Diane Davis, *Inessential Solidarity*

Trigger warning: This chapter contains somewhat detailed descriptions of gun violence and suicide on college campuses. It also mentions gun violence on elementary schools campuses.

On August 1, 2016, fifty years to the day after Charles Whitman shot and killed sixteen people on the campus of the University of Texas at Austin and injured thirty-one others, a law passed by the Texas state legislature allowing concealed handguns to be carried by license holders on public university campuses took effect.[1] The Texas State Capitol, less than two miles from the UT Austin Tower, did not seem to remark the irony or occasion. In fact, the official view given by the UT system's office of external relations was that "the campus carry legislation going into effect the same day of the 50th anniversary is a coincidence" (quoted in Eberly 2016). Of course this statement is denotatively true: the date of the two events coincides; at least at one level, this response from the Texas state legislature's office of external relations is merely begging the question. One way to understand the legislature's willful ignorance—and even insensitivity—is as part of a long history of conflict and antagonism between the University of Texas and the state government (Burr 1988; *Daily Texan* Editorial Board 2013; Nelson et al. 2013; Rainey 1971; Somers and Phelps 2018, 8), but it may also be understood as part of a larger national trend of provocations to university communities orchestrated by the gun lobby and aimed at normalizing the presence of guns in every quarter of ordinary life.

In 2016, students at the University of Texas organized a unique and headline-getting protest for the first day of class after the campus carry law's implementation, under the cheeky and assonant name "Cocks Not Glocks" (Timmons 2016b). In what might seem like a bit of a non sequitur, students strapped dildos to their backpacks, putting the new campus carry law into conversation with an older Texas state blue law prohibiting the open display of sex toys. By lampooning the law that criminalizes sexuality but permits deadly weapons, the idea was to invoke the issues of censorship and free speech, and, in the campus setting, academic freedom. The argument protestors aimed to circulate was that openly carrying the sex toys in defiance of the law was harmless, but the concealed carry of handguns on campus in *compliance* with the law presented a far more serious threat to the safety and well-being of the campus community (Dart 2016).

Alongside student protests in the months before the campus carry law in Texas (known as Senate Bill or SB 11) went into effect, three professors at UT Austin brought a lawsuit against the state and the university officials responsible for implementing the law (Waller 2018). The professors allege that SB 11 violates, among other constitutionally protected rights, their First Amendment right to academic freedom (*Glass et al.* 2016). After a judge in Texas dismissed the lawsuit, the professors escalated their complaint to the Fifth US Circuit Court of Appeals in New Orleans, where the case was ultimately dismissed (McGill 2018).

This chapter examines the public debate over campus carry laws, from the 1960s Texas law banning guns on campus to the contemporary student organization advocating to bring guns back. It connects the resonance of the 1966 Tower shooting to contemporary moments of gun violence and related provocations on the UT campus, and argues that this context is key to understanding the relationship between campus carry and academic freedom. The debate unfolds in media focused on higher education, such as online magazines like the *Chronicle of Higher Education* and *Insider Higher Ed*, as well as in student newspapers and on public or social media platforms where faculty as well as outsiders editorialize about the policies. Faculty, staff, and students who oppose campus carry laws have been frequently described in terms now quite familiar to virtually anyone who's paid attention to other campus debates in recent years: they're just too sensitive (see Valentine 2019).

As I established in chapter 1, claims about the hypersensitivity of students in particular have been in circulation now for several years on a range of campus issues, perhaps most notably trigger warnings, an issue on which student survivors of trauma have been accused of infringing on the academic freedom of their instructors by asking for notice when course material is likely to retraumatize them. In fact, the polysemy of the word *trigger* has itself created a bit of extra overlap between the campus carry debate and the trigger warnings debate as campus issues. About a month after the new gun law took effect, someone deposited shell casings on bulletin boards in several UT campus buildings, quite literally in the shadow of the Tower. The casings had small notes tucked inside that read "TRIGGERED?" (Hall 2016; see also Gerdes 2019b). I will return to this incident for further discussion a little later on. The Parlin building, where the first casings were found, is home to the Department of Rhetoric and Writing. In 1966, Austin police officer Billy Speed was shot and killed just in front of the Parlin building, near the now-former site of the Jefferson Davis statue (*Texas Standard* 2016; for another reflection on the place of Parlin in memory and rhetoric, see Boyle 2018).

Usually, arguments about sensitivity interface with other campus issues through critics who claim that students' sensitivity poses a threat to the academic freedom of the faculty. But in the case of the campus carry debate, faculty as well as students who oppose guns on campus *on the grounds of academic freedom* and free speech are the ones targeted by accusations of sensitivity. In the rare case of a contemporary campus issue where academic freedom and sensitivity appear to be aligned rather than opposed, critics' arguments against sensitivity circulate without apparent concern for academic freedom. The UT professors' lawsuit and the debate over campus carry in Texas demonstrates that the strength of attacks on sensitivity in higher education is enough to overwhelm some critics' attachment to the values of free speech and academic freedom. Austin is an especially charged site for debate over campus carry because the university itself is represented synecdochally in images as well as casual speech by the Tower, the building that Charles Whitman used in 1966 as a sniper's perch to perpetrate the first mass shooting on a college campus in US American history.

I begin my analysis of the debate over campus carry policies in Texas with a short history of college and university campus gun policies in the state.[2] I argue that the state's ban on guns on campus in the late 1960s was not a response to the Tower shooting, as one might suppose, but to student activism, especially Black student organizing that took place both before and after the Tower shooting. I then analyze the echo of racist fear underwriting Texas gun laws today, drawing on a sociological study of members of the campus gun advocacy group Students for Concealed Carry on Campus. Texas has more than once changed its campus gun laws in response to student activism, but whether it was barring guns or bringing them back, the policy changes were connected with racialized fears, and pointedly *not* with the headline-dominating school shootings, from the UT Tower to Virginia Tech, that gun advocates purported to understand as their exigence. I conclude by examining how arguments presented in the *Glass* case illuminate the condition of rhetorical sensitivity necessary to academic freedom. Sensitivity and academic freedom are and must be compatible values, and reconciling them involves recognizing and facing our own vulnerability.

A Short History

It's widely known as both stereotype and caricature that the gun culture in Texas is especially strong. Romantic (and likely apocryphal) stories about the Tower shooting contend that armed bystanders and even professors returned Whitman's fire, though even if true, such bravado seems to have neither slowed nor stopped him. Yet the strength of Texas gun fantasies like these may help to explain why the governor's report on the Tower shooting included no recommendations to ban guns from campus (Timmons 2016a). It's as if banning guns didn't cross anyone's mind in 1966. Perhaps the fantasy of heroic bystanders occluded consideration of a gun ban. Nevertheless, the year after the shooting, the Texas state legislature did try to ban guns from campus dormitories (the 1967 session was the first after the Tower shooting). But Whitman didn't live in a dorm, or keep guns there. To understand the attempt to ban guns from dorms, we have to understand more of the context the legislature was responding to at the time.

In the years immediately before the Tower shooting, civil rights activism effected major changes at universities across the country, including at UT. In 1963, in response to student protests outside their November meeting, the UT Board of Regents ruled for the removal of racial restrictions throughout the campus (Burr 1988, 14), and university-owned housing was racially integrated the following year. In 1965, student newspaper the *Daily Texan* published an editorial calling for solidarity among Black students and the development of "a racial consciousness" (25). In 1966, the year of the UT Tower shooting, the Black Panther Party for Self-Defense was founded at Merritt College in Oakland, California. In addition to establishing community programs, such as free breakfasts and health clinics, the Black Panthers laid claim to the right of using guns as tools of self-defense, explicitly contesting the US American norm that reserves this right for mainly white men. Their influence was felt in student and activist groups across the country.

The year after the Tower shooting, in April 1967, chairman of the Student Nonviolent Coordinating Committee Stokely Carmichael (later known by the name Kwame Ture) gave a speech on the UT campus in which he "spoke about the black power movement and criticized the 'white racist press' for its unfair reporting" (Burr 1988, 25). In May 1967, a dorm at Texas State University in Houston was the scene of a violent police raid, widely reported at the time as a Black student riot. A police officer was killed by a bullet later determined to be ricochet from Houston police gunfire (LaRotta 2017). Four hundred and eighty-eight students were arrested, and the "TSU Five," who were charged with inciting the riot, were released due to insufficient evidence. In the 1967 legislative session, the ban on guns in dorms failed, but the legislature did pass a law allowing campus security officers to be recognized as sworn police officers, permitting them to carry guns on campus (Pennie 2017, 58).

Meanwhile in Austin, Black student organizations garnered public attention by focusing on the failure of the university to recruit Black athletes. In 1968, only a few months after the assassination of Martin Luther King Jr., the student group Afro-Americans for Black Liberation helped establish two new programs in Afro-American studies at UT (Burr 1988, 26). Black students were gaining ground in the fight for civil rights on campus. After a controversial meeting of leaders from Students for Democratic Society in March 1969 (Segalman and Segalman 1969), UT police were concerned about "the presence of armed white and black radicals on campus" (Timmons 2016a). By the time the state legislature met again in 1969, they were ready to enact a total campus ban on guns (Timmons 2016a). An Institute for Public Affairs report on the 61st legislative session described the bill as a "response to a growing concern about campus violence," noting (strangely, given the incident at TSU two years earlier) that "Texas has thus far been spared any militant student unrest" (Institute of Public Affairs 1970, 28).

The timing of legislative action to ban guns on campus coincides not only with the Tower shooting, which seems to have caused barely a ripple of reflection about the role of guns on campus, but also with the growing solidarity and mobilization for social action among Black students across the state and the nation. The timing of the ban, situated in the context of campus politics in the late 1960s, suggests that it wasn't the Tower shooting that catalyzed the Texas legislature to ban guns, but radical student activism. The question of allowing guns on campus has historically been not only a *provocation to* student activism but a *response to* the activism of Black students.

A Persistent Theme

It's said that history repeats itself. In the case of campus guns laws in the state of Texas, history also reversed itself. The legislature disarmed the campus because it was afraid of the possibility of armed and organized Black students in the 1960s; but in the 2010s, the legislature rearmed the campus in response to the agitating and organizing of white students. Perhaps because the incidence of campus shootings has only become more frequent and spectacular since the turn of the millennium, it would be easy to think that those college students who do support campus carry laws[3] are concerned about their ability to protect themselves in, as we now casually call it, an active shooter situation. To be sure, some have made that claim—though research into the beliefs and arguments advanced by student advocates for campus carry contradicts it (see

Couch 2014). Evidence also contradicts the realism of the belief that a good guy with a gun is the only thing that can stop a bad guy with a gun. Setting aside for the moment the few recent times that active shooters have been slowed down or disrupted by the intervention of unarmed civilians—often by veterans or young people with military commitments ahead of them (Britzky 2019)—recall that when a shooter opened fire on the Umpqua Community College campus in Oregon in 2015, a state that did then and does now allow concealed carry on campus, Air Force veteran John Parker Jr. told news media that he and other armed veterans who were with him chose not to pursue the shooter because "we could have opened ourselves up to be potential targets ourselves, and not knowing where SWAT was, their response time, they wouldn't know who we were. And if we had our guns ready to shoot, they could think that we were bad guys" (Boggioni 2015; see also Kennedy, de Yoanna, and Kehrt 2022). Like many other active shooter incidents, the UCC incident ended when the shooter died by suicide. Perhaps advocates of campus carry laws believe that in the midst of such violence and uncertainty they'd somehow make smarter tactical decisions than trained vets like Parker. (For an excellent rhetorical analysis of this fantasy, see Cryer 2020.)

Such self-certainty unwarranted by facts or experience would not be inconsistent with the other beliefs of campus carry advocates. For his dissertation research at Texas A&M University in 2014, sociologist Todd Couch conducted thirty interviews with members of the contemporary group Students for Concealed Carry on Campus (SCCC). Couch found a widespread and "very intense pro-white/anti-other racial framing guiding much of SCCC membership" (ii). Couch asked his interview subjects about how they got involved with the group and to describe their beliefs about concealed carry on campus, their personal carrying practices, and their history with firearms as well as their desire to obtain a concealed handgun license (CHL). At the close of his interviews, Couch also asked his subjects to describe the demographics of their SCCC chapters. When asked about the racial homogeneity of their chapters, Couch's respondents often became incoherent, pausing for a long time or searching for words (79). If they claimed that their group only reflected the demographics of the larger campus community, Couch confronted them with recent demographic information about their campus, which consistently demonstrated far more diversity than respondents had claimed that there was. In these instances, respondents expressed disbelief and urged the interviewer to check his facts. They described their (failed) attempts to get women and people of color to join the groups and even claimed *their group* was discriminated against *because* its membership consists mainly of white men.

This persecution-complex perspective was not held unanimously, however. The only two women who agreed to be interviewed for Couch's research did describe their SCCC chapters as having a "good ol' boy vibe," but they actually seem to pride themselves on not being overly sensitive—on being able to tolerate the pervasive sexist and racist jokes, attributing such joking to boys being boys (80). In contrast, the military veterans who were interviewed commented openly on the overt racism of SCCC members. One veteran respondent commented, "I came to see that the kids here were just concerned about not getting robbed by minorities. That's all they would talk about" (87). The veterans who participated in Couch's study were so put off by the other members' racism that they were discouraged by their experience from recommending the group to others, and it seems all of the veteran participants had stopped attending or left the group altogether by the time interviews took place (81–88).

Couch's findings confirm the investment of SCCC members in white supremacy far beyond denialism or dim awareness of the racial homogeneity of their groups. Couch's respondents consistently testified to their fears of racialized others as the main motivation for their desire to carry concealed handguns, not only on campus specifically but as part of an undifferentiated right to carry at all times. One interviewee directly disclosed, "We're not concerned so much about school shootings. The likelihood of that sort of thing is pretty slim. Those aren't the people we're really concerned about. We're more interested in individual self-defense. When I'm walking home at night there are always these . . . well just to be honest black guys outside the store by my house" (55–56). Couch elicited this comment from his respondent over the phone; Couch, a multiracial Black man, sometimes met his interview subjects in person, sometimes spoke with them by videoconference, and sometimes spoke with them over the phone. He organized their comments into categories ranging from hard racial framing like the comment I have quoted earlier to soft or socially permitted racial framing, such as fear of and complaints about immigration, or about crime in predominantly Black neighborhoods, to color-blind racial framing, where the dynamic of race is minimized or denied, as in the fumbling responses to Couch's demographic inquiries. Couch notes that hard racial framing only appeared in interviews conducted at a distance without cameras (51).

Couch's study, which crossed campuses and regions of the United States, demonstrates that anti-Black and anti-immigrant racism broadly informs the views of students who are organized in favor of campus carry across the country. Some respondents openly articulated their racialized fears as part of a culture war in which white US American masculinity is viewed as under attack not only by men of color but by feminists and queer people as well as gun control advocates (57–58). Although respondents tended to displace assertions of white vulnerability onto women (i.e., saying they want to carry at all times in order to be able to protect their girlfriends, wives, or daughters), their attachment to guns enables respondents to repair their masculinity by disavowing the very fantasy of vulnerability that underwrites their desire for guns (see Rood 2019, 2020). As Couch points out, the fear of being victimized is articulated as an assertion that carrying a gun enables one to choose *not* to be a victim (109). The fantasy effectively sublimates an experience of sensitivity into an assertion of invulnerability.

Couch concludes with a clarion call for campus administrators to consider how the implementation of campus carry laws will affect their students of color, "since they are the group/individuals framed by most of the members of SCCC as threatening and warranting the loosening of gun control to allow for firearms on campus" (127, 133). I would add that other people of color who are members of the campus community, including staff as well as faculty of color, are disproportionately exposed to the possible negative impacts of an armed campus environment in which they are viewed, especially by gun advocates, as not belonging (see Ore 2017). UT's Institute for Urban Policy Research and Analysis polled registered Texas voters in March 2016 and found that "the majority of Black (79%) and Latino voters (66%) oppose[d] allowing concealed handgun licensees to carry handguns on public university campuses, while less than half of White voters (47%) opposed" the policy (Cokley 2016, 2). Though by no means a perfect proxy for the views of faculty and staff, the data do indicate a wide gap among racial demographic groups regarding campus carry. A statement issued by UT's African American and African Diaspora Department, noting the commonplace nature of threats and harassment targeting Black faculty, argues that "in the presence of firearms the probability that bullets will find us is higher than for any other campus population" (quoted in Somers and Phelps 2018, 12).

How deeply animating is the fear of racialized others in the history of guns and the University of Texas? In *Towers of Rhetoric: Memory and Invention*, Rosa Eberly briefly recounts arguments that put the UT Tower shooting in this precise context: "In addition to Whitman's family stress and substance abuse, historian Doug Rassinow, in his book *The Politics of Authenticity*, argued persuasively that Charles Whitman was also a racist, inflamed by white supremacists, who chose his victims not randomly but for specific reasons. Rassinow describes Whitman as 'a student with strongly racist views and apparently with ties to the Minutemen' (175). TimeLife's *True Crime: Mass Murderers* quotes anecdotes reported by Whitman's friends of his bullying African American students and international students." These claims belie the narrative, which now commonly attaches to many a modern-day mass shooting, that the motives of such violence are mysterious and unknowable. In 2016, to commemorate the Tower shooting fifty years on, the *Texas Standard* radio program created an online multimedia documentary, catachrestically named "Out of the Blue."[4] The title is a misnomer, though it fits a widely held public narrative. Understanding the UT Tower shooting as a random act of violence enabled the widespread and long-lived denialism about the central role white masculinity played in this violence. The smiling portrait of the shooter in coat and tie, refrains about his military service and his youthful achievement of the Eagle Scout rank—the image of the shooter as an all-American boy (at age 25) was constructed and recirculated *because* of what it elided: aggrieved whiteness; wounded masculinity; violence that at least began as targeted, first, against the women in the shooter's life.[5] After the Columbine shooting in 1999, both Orlando Patterson and Gloria Steinem identified this same denialist dynamic at work in contemporary popular media coverage (Patterson 1999; Steinem 1999). When white masculinity, however aggressively dysfunctional, is normalized and venerated in US American culture, its role in the spectacular violence of mass shooting is mystified.

Students for Concealed Carry on Campus was formed the day after the Virginia Tech shooting in 2007, but whether this means the group is a response to fear about students' vulnerability to campus shootings—or strategic opportunism—ought to be viewed as an open question. Journalist Adam Weinstein argues in a 2015 article that the conservative Blackwell Leadership Institute helped train campus leaders and paid organizers to seed SCCC chapters across the country (see also Somers and Phelps 2018, 3)—meaning that SCCC chapters, while they do engage in student activism, do not reflect a genuine grassroots student movement. According to Weinstein's reporting, campus carry activism is part of a larger right-wing strategy in which state bills like SB 11, even when they don't pass, can be used to identify moderate Republicans vulnerable to primary challengers. Strategists are aware that securing changes in state law is not the only effect of debating campus carry legislation around the country. Such debates can be used to inflame racist and xenophobic passions, and to drag the right-wing of US American politics further and further to the right.

Aftermath at UT in 2016

After SB 11 took effect in Texas, the *New York Times* interviewed, among other stakeholders at the University of Texas, a graduate student who chose to meet the writer and photographer in the campus library because he lived with housemates that he thought wouldn't like his views on guns. Whether he should have disclosed to his housemates that he kept firearms in the house they shared, the student clearly violated the new law by displaying his gun for the photographer to document while he was in the campus library (Phillips 2016; see also Timmons 2016b). Published just three days after the start of fall classes, the *NYT* photo documents a student who is licensed to carry a concealed handgun violating the *concealed* stipulation of the law. Presumably, the library in question is the main Perry-Castañeda Library, where less than six years prior, an armed student who had walked to the library from across campus, firing random shots on his way but not apparently targeting others, died by suicide on the library's top floor. When the campus went into a more than three-hour lockdown while SWAT teams investigated classrooms and campus buildings, concerned by conflicting reports that there might be a second shooter (there wasn't), the UT chapter of SCCC had to cancel their on-campus venue for a lecture by the author of a specious book called *More Guns, Less Crime*[6] (on the event cancellation, see Goldberg 2010). I doubt that the graduate student who displayed his weapon to the *NYT* photographer was sensitive to, let alone aware of, this resonance: the fact that the last known time a student bore a firearm into that campus library, he had terrorized the campus community and then died there. I can tell you that as both a rhetorician and a graduate of the University of Texas, I am tuned in to such resonances, and I hope that sharing them here—drawing a line between many moments connected to the same topos—will make the affective and psychological landscape of that topos more legible. That this resonance, or we might say coincidence, is lost on some does not mean it isn't exerting an affective force: "There is a zone of undecidability that invests the difference between knowledge and ignorance" (Ronell 2002, 118).[7] The topos may be physical and geographical, but it's also emotional. Perhaps the topos remembers and makes its history felt, even when the project of public remembrance lies long neglected (for more on UT's resistance to remembering the Tower shooting, and on teaching as a rhetorical intervention, see Eberly 2004).

The grad student's casual violation of the new campus carry law was not the only breach in the responsible gun behavior that the law's advocates had promised. I turn back now to the shell casings found in Parlin Hall and other nearby buildings in September 2016. There were at least three. The first one found was placed atop a bulletin board, above a flyer for the group Gun Free UT advertising the group's Peace Zone workshop. The flyer was defaced with text reading: "In the land of the pigs, the butcher is king. oink . . . oink . . . oink . . ." Some readers may think that the note ("TRIGGERED?") in the shell casing is ambiguous, an underarticulated argument if an argument at all. The note reads quite clearly as a taunt directed at members of UT's community who object to the presence of guns on campus. Taken together with the writing on the flyer, the taunt also resonates as a threat. Here are the suppressed premises in the argument: *If you don't carry a gun, you're as vulnerable as a pig to a butcher. If that claim upsets you, you're too sensitive. Being sensitive makes you vulnerable. You could protect yourself—if you were carrying a gun.* I suppose that is how the Texas state legislature would like you to compensate for your feelings of exposedness. The note in the shell casing (dare I say) weaponizes the jeering critique of sensitivity—a critique that in 2016 had been incubating in the trigger warnings debate for more than two years—and mobilizes its associated premises with the distinct aim of intimidating the display's targeted audience. Such intimidation presents a real threat to academic freedom—one that, though difficult to precisely measure (see Esch, Jones, and Roediger 2018), has begun to be explored in the courts.

The Case for Academic Freedom

In 2016, Dr. Jennifer Lynn Glass, Dr. Lisa Moore, and Dr. Mia Carter—three professors at UT Austin—sued the university, the board of regents, and the attorney general over SB 11; their main claim is that the campus carry law, and its specific implementation at UT, violates their First Amendment right to academic freedom. Although the case was dismissed by the district court, and again on appeal to the Fifth Circuit (Largey 2018), the claims in the suit are still worth examining because they articulate academic freedom *with* sensitivity rather than against it. The complaint was brought to a district court in Texas before the law took effect. Initially, the plaintiffs sought an injunction against the university's decision to allow guns in classrooms. In theory, UT might have opted to allow teachers to decide for themselves whether to allow guns in their classrooms. But while the law allowed schools to create their own rules for implementation, it does not allow rules that would "generally prohibit" guns on campus, a provision that has been understood to handcuff schools over the specific issue of classrooms. Despite their inability to recommend excluding guns from classrooms, the campus carry working group at UT unanimously expressed fear that the new law would chill the free speech of both students and faculty (a legal point also argued in Lewis and De Luna 2016). The Faculty Council also passed a resolution calling for a classroom exclusion.

Among the plaintiffs' other claims is an equal protection argument predicated on the fact that nearly all private colleges and universities, as well as many locations on the UT Austin campus *other than* classrooms, are excluded from the requirement to allow concealed carry; plaintiffs argue that no rational basis clearly divides those locations where guns are allowed from those where they are not. For example, private offices may be excluded, but shared offices, such as those often assigned to graduate teaching assistants, cannot be excluded, even if every occupant wants their office excluded. Plaintiffs also advanced a due process claim based on the attorney general's threat to punish professors who do try to prohibit or even discourage CHL holders from bringing guns into the classroom. The suit also contained the novel claim of a Second Amendment violation, arguing that the licensure requirements in Texas, as well as in the forty-three other states from which Texas recognizes CHLs, are not "well-regulated," because "there has not been the imposition of proper discipline and training" (*Glass et al.* 2016, 5). In 2021, Texas did away with even its meager license requirements (four hours of training, a written exam, and a proficiency demonstration) for anyone over the age of 21.

In 2017, the American Association of University Professors (AAUP) filed a brief in support of the professors' appeal (Flaherty 2017b). Their review of the case law surrounding academic freedom, especially as it touches on speech in the classroom, argues that a law's chilling effect on free speech is determined by the standard of whether "a person of ordinary firmness" would be deterred from exercising their rights (Brief for the AAUP 2017, 18). The brief then presents social science research on the widespread opposition to campus carry among students, faculty, and staff, also citing a joint statement of opposition to such laws signed by the AAUP, the American Federation of Teachers, the Association of American Colleges and Universities, and the Association of Governing Boards of Universities and Colleges (Brief 2017, 20). Because the *Glass* plaintiffs each teach courses involving controversial social issues, the AAUP argues that the court should recognize the professors as the experts on how the possible presence of handguns in their classrooms would alter the exercise of academic freedom in their courses: "Just as chemists best determine which chemicals are combustible, individual faculty must be able to decide that the ideas in their courses are particularly volatile, warranting the exclusion of guns" (24). The academic discussion of controversial topics, which often challenges students' dearly held beliefs, is only possible if the classroom is understood as a site reserved for the rhetorical practice of negotiating disagreement. Even the possibility that one's interlocutors may have a concealed handgun pierces this rhetorical space by placing a limit on one's willingness to risk provoking anger in someone who may have a lethal weapon. There is a demonstrated chilling effect accompanying such a breach of a sensitive space (see Jones and Horan 2019). The presence of guns intensifies one's vulnerability to violence. The *Glass* plaintiffs and the AAUP brief contend that guns and rhetoric can't coexist freely; the presence of guns in the classroom dissolves it as a safe space and diminishes academic freedom.

It might seem strange for a court to adjudicate these claims about the rhetorical nature of a college classroom, and about the relationship between rhetoric and violence—especially since courts, like many other public sites of debate and deliberation in the United States, ban firearms. In a law review article entitled "Guns and Academic Freedom," Aurora Temple Barnes argues that two Supreme Court cases clearly indicate a First Amendment right to academic freedom (*Sweezy* and *Keyishian*), and that this right extends to both institutions and to individual professors (2017, 23). But Barnes cautions that the legal threshold for harm to academic freedom has not been clearly established. Patricia Somers and Nicholas Phelps, writing in the AAUP's *Journal of Academic Freedom*, report that "faculty have been injured psychologically and taken specific steps to avoid harm. . . . They modify their classroom content and their delivery. They modify their interactions with students outside the classroom" (2018, 13). The antagonism of the reactionary conservative state legislature and attorney general toward the public university and its faculty suggests that the fear, stress, and anxiety caused by SB 11 (10), and the exposure to intimidation and harassment caused by public opposition to the law (12), may be among its intended effects.

Somers and Phelps interviewed 140 UT Austin faculty members around the time that SB 11 took effect, and they observed a shift in tenor of even casual conversations between faculty members. Instead of talking about "research, vacations, or classes," one faculty member remarked, she and her colleagues were preoccupied with "issues such as the 'difference between a loaded weapon and chambered round,' 'the difference between prohibiting and discouraging weapons in the classroom,' and mourning the loss of academic freedom and faculty governance" (2018, 5). The respondents linked their concerns about safety to their own memories of UT Austin as a topos of violence[8] in a way I found striking: "Many of the general comments about safety were punctuated by references to violent incidents on campus"—and here they go on to describe not only those incidents of gun violence that I have mentioned here, but also two murders committed on campus (one in 2016 and one in 2017), as well as an off-campus shooting at a fraternity party.[9] The authors remark, "As the participants related these scenarios we could visualize these 'flashbulb' memories perfectly" (5). A similar experience inflected my writing of this chapter, which at times felt as if it wanted to become a memorialization of gun traumas at my alma mater. These traumas are collective, inflicted on a campus community that spans many times, places, and relations to the university. They are not easily remembered, especially when the institution and the state wishes them to be forgotten. They are not easy to remember, because trauma is a flashbulb, sudden and blinding. But neither are they easy to forget.

These traumas should be remembered, remarked, and understood as the context for both gun policy and the practice (and limitation) of academic freedom at UT Austin. Texans had to mark the fiftieth anniversary of the first mass school shooting by submitting to allow concealed handguns into that school's classrooms. As teachers, we ought not to forget that a generation of our students has grown up rehearsing active shooter drills, watching as the accelerated frequency of mass shootings diminishes their purported mystery. Although the likelihood of facing a school shooting may remain statistically small, our students as well as our colleagues are affected by gun violence in myriad other places, too: in our neighborhoods and homes; in the forms of intimidation, abuse, accidents, and suicide (see Rood 2019, 5). School violence, or even the threat of it, operates to destabilize the social bond of trust in being together that is presupposed, uniquely, by public education. By exploiting sensitivity as a target for predation, the rhetorical relation that depends on it is jeopardized, and members of the public are more easily fractured and isolated from one another. If academic freedom matters to us, we will have to embrace, in its defense, the sensitive nature of our classrooms and our communities. We are vulnerable to violence, and to the threat of violence, and to the limits inscribed on what can be thought, said, and heard by symbolic violence (see Eberly 2018, chapter 6). Yet this sensitivity to affection in language is also what makes it possible for us to study, teach, and learn.

Coda

I'm no longer a Longhorn, but for several years I remained a Texan, joining the faculty at Texas Tech University. I stopped reflecting the Red Raiders' school spirit hand sign—"guns up"—to the parking attendants on campus in 2017, after I was locked down in my office while teaching an online class. An armed student murdered an officer inside the campus police station, then fled across the campus. When it happened, my grad students and I were discussing Diane Davis's case for a rhetoric of responsibility (2010). Davis argues that we are brought into being as subjects in language through a preoriginary responsibility for others. We can feel this responsibility, she suggests, through being faced with the possibility of death. The finitude of life—the fact that there are limits—is what makes it possible for me to be affected by others. I become a rhetorical subject, Davis argues, *in response* to the difference from me of those who affect me.

My students were talking about whether anything other than death could awaken us to this exposedness, this finitude, whether anything other than death could lead us to embrace our sensitivity to rhetorical affection and the responsibility that Davis argues comes with it.

I was saying, when a student alerted me to the lockdown order, that perhaps even spectacular violence *does not* awaken us. The possibility of death is a vulnerability, and when it confronts us, we may refuse to face it, and refuse to face the fact that we share this vulnerability, irreparably, with others.

Facing our own vulnerability is not easy, and for all the talk of how we need to work harder to understand each other across political differences, it's not actually that hard to understand wanting to arm yourself against your own vulnerability, or wanting to blame someone whose difference from you makes you feel affected and exposed—too sensitive. I don't think understanding is the rhetorical problem here. It's indifference. Perhaps the harshest lesson of school shootings, from the Tower shooting to Uvalde, is the political force of indifference. Unthinkable violence is naturalized by the ideology of those who stand to profit off it and of those who cannot stand to contemplate responding to it. Davis writes that "indifference is the luxury of exposed existents who are not *faced* with the fact of their exposedness" (2010, 10). I shut my office door, shut off the light, and silently sent text messages to my wife, my parents, my colleagues in the building with me. Being exposed makes us responsible to one another. The violence was actually already over by the time the lockdown started; I hadn't *really* been in harm's way. But I'd lost the will, the next day or two, to wave even a symbolic hand gun at others with whom I shared another Texas campus, where the law welcomes handguns so long as they're concealed.

Conclusion

Sensitivity's Rhetorical Force

> We are beings who have to be addressed in order to live, who are addressed by others through language or through other signifying practices, including touch and noise, and that without those forms of enabling address, we do not really survive. . . . Without address, there is no survival.

> **Judith Butler, interview with Sara Ahmed**

Time and again, sensitivity has been the central target of opposition to contemporary student activism, and academic freedom has been made to play its foil. Examining the way public debates about student activism treat sensitivity shows us how effectively appeals to academic freedom could recruit adherents from all points on the ideological spectrum. Yet when academic freedom more clearly aligns *with* sensitivity, as in opposition to campus carry laws, or when the neoliberal interests of the university or a state legislature are at stake, the value of academic freedom seems to diminish, and appeals that rely on it fall by the wayside in favor of those arguments that make sensitivity into a target.

When I began the research that would become this project in late 2014, tuning in to the public conversation about trigger warnings as a form of student activism gave me the opportunity to notice how accusations that students were just being too sensitive seemed to be coming from all directions—that is, it was not only right-wing pundits who wanted students to simply buck up and grow a thicker skin: leftist, queer, and feminist scholars joined the chorus. Wondering why led me to investigate the appeal to academic freedom, with its unique connection to higher education, to distinguish it from appeals to free speech on other kinds of cultural and activist issues. Then I looked for where these appeals would be repeated: appeals to academic freedom, yes, but specific invocations of trigger warnings, as well, surfaced time and again in connection to progressive student activism, from debates about safe spaces to Title IX policy, and with a twist, in debates about campus carry laws, where suddenly students weren't the only ones who were too sensitive, and academic freedom was easily subordinated to other types of freedom—namely, those imagined to be enshrined in the Second Amendment.

When I first started researching and writing about the trigger warnings debate, I thought that critiques of students' sensitivity were misdirected and overly harsh. The process of examining how these critiques have circulated and evolved, appearing in other student activist issues, and even reversing themselves when ideologically convenient, leads me now to view critiques of sensitivity as part of a coordinated right-wing campaign aimed at fracturing solidarity between students and faculty and between members of the higher education community and the wider public. To call this attack "coordinated" is not to imply that there's one coherent playbook or author; ideology moves much more fluidly than that. But the playbook has been in full view for a number of years now, repeated as a reactionary response to #MeToo, wokeness, Black Lives Matter, first callout culture and then cancel culture. If we don't bother to observe the underlying theories of rhetoric (however unstated or unexamined) that make sensitivity seem only to be a feature of weakness, then we will miss its damaging sequelae as the force, harm, violence, and trauma of language circulates in our communities unchecked. On the other hand, if we pay attention to claims about sensitivity and choose to center our theory on our exposedness to rhetorical affection, we have a chance to better grasp the effectivity of language and to better respond to those who are working to demonstrate and combat injustice, especially those who are our students.

While not all of the issues analyzed in this book come from public universities, the publicity of higher education is nevertheless a significant part of its concern. For some, the democratizing of student populations (even at private institutions) is a problem of diluting the elite cultural function of higher education. Of course for writing teachers, documenting the history—and intervening against the elitist impulses—of higher education is our disciplinary heritage. Access, inclusion, equity, and diversity have become bywords at many corporate institutions even beyond the university. Yet they are also the cynosures we must follow in pursuit of a more just future for higher education, a future in which higher education is more hospitable to those whom it has historically excluded.

Education is more than a private, individual good; education is a common good, ideally benefiting all members of a democratic citizenry by developing our abilities not only to see the validity in perspectives that differ from our own but to ethically and responsibility negotiate our differences even when they cannot be reconciled. Public education, and not just higher education, is a culture war target in no small part because of its potential role in a vigorous deliberative democracy. When academic freedom is propped up against sensitivity, it risks becoming private, the sole province of the individual teacher or learner, on whose rights the sensitivity of others is said to impinge. But sensitivity as I have theorized it here is instead the very rhetorical structure that makes it possible to learn, to address others, to negotiate difference together.

Sensitivity marks a place in public argument where our vulnerability to one another as rhetorical existents gets denied and even buried. It names an irremissible exposedness that brings us into relation as subjects in language. Before symbolic persuasion, before thinking and knowing, even before the experience of being, a rhetorical sensitivity obtains, opening us to existence as rhetorical subjects. To inquire into rhetorical sensitivity demands a rethinking of affect, of its force and potential trauma. What I hope to have shown in this work is that rhetorical sensitivity is always already freighted with compelling affective force. It is a force we may describe as moving, shattering, even traumatic, operating at a presubjective level. Outside of the domain of symbolic exchange, prior to the agentive power of the rhetorical subject, our sensitivity to rhetorical affection *makes us*, and makes us vulnerable. But this sensitivity is also the condition of possibility for our reception of and response to the world.

The value of looking to student insight about academic cultures and practices is, in the first place, that many student activists are focused on just these things. Students' experiences of our classrooms, pedagogies, departments and programs, norms, and expectations are material—that is, they aren't *merely* symbolic or emotional or in some way purely abstract. Their scholarly work but also their scholarships, access to student loans, ability to live on campus, and many other ordinary aspects of their daily lives are organized, through the bureaucracy of the institution, in part by the beliefs and practices of their professors. Sometimes we joke that the extent of our power does not go far enough: if only we could convince these students to, say, read the syllabus! And yet our choices also help determine whether their experience of higher education will be one that welcomes them in their alterity, their differences from each other and from us, or one that alienates them, even to a breaking point.

Without this study of sensitivity in the context of student activism, we might not be able to see the pattern of arguments that yoke academic freedom to a critique of sensitivity, nor the exact moment when academic freedom will be discarded by potential allies when the politics split a different way. This study makes plain the potential violence that language can enact, even in the most mundane, formal, or sanctioned settings you can imagine. Student activists are attuned to this potential for violence, and they routinely meet it with clarity about the difference between exercising freedom of speech and amplifying or even elevating speech that will do harm. This difference is the heart of the debate about deplatforming (or "no-platforming") campus guest speakers, yet another campus issue on which students' sensitivity is commonly critiqued, and students infantilized. Aaron R. Hanlon (2017) argues that when students work to disinvite incendiary speakers, activists are well within their own free speech rights to criticize and respond to the invitations. Although Hanlon doesn't think disruptive tactics are particularly effective, he makes it clear that not every speaker deserves a campus platform. Debate over the criteria and value of a given candidate is entirely appropriate for campus stakeholders, and that includes students. Brian Bailie (2020) details both the tactics such debates should employ and the importance of refusing white supremacist speakers a platform: their views should not be elevated to "the status of a rational argument that must be heard." We should want our students to deplatform and contest genocidal propagandists, on campus and off. No matter how well dressed or civil they appear.

The failures of US American universities to object to Nazism and anti-intellectualism has already had a legitimating force, reaching as far back as the 1930s. Stephen H. Norwood (2011) details how university presidents flouted boycotts of German travel, ignored Nazi book burnings and denied their seriousness, and defended the speaking invitations extended by US American universities to Nazis, treating them as distinguished guests of the university. Yet Jewish scholars and students, simply by existing, were viewed as inciting controversy and refused a campus platform; refugees, when they were admitted to US American universities, were limited by quota and even sometimes depended on student fundraisers to cover their housing and tuition (Norwood 2011). We don't have to keep repeating our mistakes. In fact, preliminary research into deplatforming toxic communities online shows that moderating discussion forums can significantly reduce both the number of posts and active users, as well as diminish the attraction of newcomers (Ribeiro, Jhaver, and Zannettou et al. 2021)—that is, it can make recruiting harder for white supremacists. Moderation by qualified experts is the bedrock of scholarly peer review. It is a scholarly standard that helps legitimate academic freedom, and it ought to be applied widely in academic forums.

It is my hope that *Sensitive Rhetorics* will first of all give stakeholders in higher education a reason to rethink commonplaces about student sensitivity, not only their accuracy and utility as descriptions of student activists but also their effectivity in shaping the direction of policy debates as well as the climate in which today's students are pursuing their education. And that not only on campus but in the wider culture as well: controversies about whether to devote public resources to amplify white supremacist propaganda and literal sexual harassment aren't limited to colleges and universities. There's a commonplace that higher education is a microcosm of public life. To specify it in this case, the arguments developed and tested in campus environments migrate into other public debates, about laws and politics, about sexual power in the workplace, about K–12 education policy and about gun policy (and these are the same thing), and about stand-up comedy and video games and social media and other forms of entertainment and art. Sensitivity has been targeted as a liability; I hope this book has shown how sensitivity may be affirmed instead as an ineradicable asset and a condition of possibility for ethical rhetorical relationships.

Those of us committed to the value of academic freedom and to its place in the education of a democratic citizenry should not be persuaded by critiques of sensitivity but instead make sensitivity the basis of a more ethical rhetorical theory. Sensitive rhetorics can reshape these debates about university policy and culture, putting the power that each of us holds to both wound and to harm one another at the center of rhetorical theory.

Notes

Introduction. Being Sensitive and Rhetorical Being

1. For an examination of responsibility as a key tension in the relationships between teachers and students, see Eric Detweiler's *Responsible Pedagogy*.

2. For a thorough treatment of the history and strategy behind advocacy for viewpoint diversity, see Bradford Vivian, *Campus Misinformation*.

3. Though our usages of *vulnerability* differs significantly, the importance of this term in rhetoric and writing studies can be traced at least back to Ken Macrorie in *A Vulnerable Teacher* (1974). For more on the political uses of vulnerability, see Katie Oliviero, *Vulnerability Politics* (2018).

4. Literature professor Benjamin Balthaser has called for greater specificity in discussions of "the university" (a term I invoke often in this book), such as distinguishing between institutional types, and between faculty and administration, for example (Balthaser 2022). I completed my PhD at the University of Texas at Austin, a public flagship with a long history of conflict between the university and the state government (see chapter 4). I view higher education as a right and as a common good, and I view its systematic defunding as an attack on its capacity to develop a democratic citizenry. These perspectives shape my use of "the university" throughout this book.

5. Just when I thought the trigger warnings discourse was dead or retired, *Insider Higher Ed*, the *Chronicle*, and the *New Yorker* all published articles reanimating the trigger warnings debate in late 2021 (Bugeja 2021; Gersen 2021; Khalid and Synder 2021). Khalid and Snyder reiterate their critique in another *Chronicle* piece from 2023, claiming that trigger warnings are part of a package of inclusion policies they deem overtly opposed to academic freedom.

Chapter 1. Sensitive Students

1. My use of "affection" here follows Diane Davis, who ties the action of affecting to the state of being affected, as in this passage from *Inessential Solidarity*: "If rhetorical practices work by managing to have an effect on others, then an always prior openness to the other's affection is its first requirement: the 'art' of rhetoric can be effective only among affectable existents" (3).

2. For more on the relationship between academic freedom, teaching, and students, see Crowley (1998, chapter 10), Boland (2007), and Reichman (2015); for a strong case linking the practice of teaching and accommodation, see Womack (2017).

3. Vivian (2023) addresses methodological issues with and subsequent misrepresentations of several similar studies on trigger warnings in his fourth chapter, "Pseudoscience."

4. See Bedera (2021), who argues for other pedagogical practices that might better center the needs of survivors of sexual violence, specifically by preventing the repeat trauma of institutional betrayal; see also Grayson (2020), who criticizes the potential for using trigger warnings to institute a "politeness protocol," especially surrounding issues of racial justice.

5. Vivian (2023) effectively rebuts claims that Yiannopoulos and his contemporaries offer students "diverse viewpoints" in his fifth chapter, "Mobs and Shutdowns."

6. Here I cite Avital Ronell, concerned that it would be intellectually dishonest of me not to, yet cognizant of an NYU Title IX investigation finding her responsible for sexual harassment (made public in 2018). The debacle of Ronell's Title IX case stemmed in part from her refusal to accept the very type of ethical responsibility that her scholarship so carefully elucidates.

7. Sonja K. Foss and Cindy L. Griffin (1995) did make such a claim, contending that persuasion entails a violent desire to dominate and change others, and proposing instead an invitational rhetoric. In centering the autonomy of the individual, invitational rhetoric is not consonant with the constitutive exposedness that sensitivity describes. Building on Foss and Griffin's critique (among others'), Brooke Rollins contends that violence and rhetoric are both instruments "designed to *move* others" (2009, 540). She concludes, however, that rhetoric's forcefulness shows individual autonomy to be illusory (a claim that resonates with the theory of sensitivity presented here). For a treatment of the long-standing opposition between rhetoric and violence, and of the way violence is circulated rhetorically, see Megan Eatman, *Ecologies of Harm*.

8. Note that "violent" often appears as a descriptor in definitions of the verb *shock*, as in *Merriam-Webster*'s "a sudden or violent mental or emotional

disturbance" (*Merriam-Webster* 2017) or in the OED's "to come into violent contact," and compare "to wound the feelings of" (*Oxford English Dictionary* 2017).

9. John Palfrey outlines a similar argument in his book *Safe Spaces, Brave Spaces: Diversity and Free Expression in Education* (2017).

Chapter 2. Sensitive Subjects

1. The universalizing effect of a purportedly neutral rhetorical figure has long been a problem for feminist antiviolence movements: see Richie (2000). Although not considered to be nationally representative, a 2007 study by the Bureau of Justice Statistics found that one in five college women had experienced completed or attempted sexual assault since starting college (Krebs, Lindquist, and Warner et al., 2007). A more recent study released in 2016 suggested that campus sexual assaults were vastly underreported (40 reported by Clery Act standards at nine schools studied; 2,380 reported by survey participants at the same schools; Krebs, Lindquist, and Berzofsky et al. 2016).

2. For scholarship in rhetoric that directly addresses sexual assault and the reparative rhetorical work of survival, see LeMesurier (2019).

3. In an article in the *Yale Law Journal*, MacKinnon (2016) argues that the "deliberate indifference" standard is grossly insufficient in the judicial context for the equality objective of Title IX. Although MacKinnon is critical of the limited administrative enforcement power of the Office for Civil Rights, she praises the strength of those regulations that DeVos effectively gutted (2100).

4. The *New York Times* ran a story on Ronell's case under the headline "What Happens to #MeToo When a Feminist Is the Accused?" (Greenberg 2018), echoing Jane Gallop's 1997 book title, *Feminist Accused of Sexual Harassment*.

5. In his book *Sex Panic Rhetorics, Queer Interventions*, Ian Barnard draws on Kipnis's book as evidence of "an increasing infantilization of US college students" (138), a dynamic whose racialized dimensions I explore in chapter 3. Barnard argues that infantilizing college students contributes to what he terms "pedagogy panics," which often make queer teachers, people, and books into public targets. I don't disagree with this conclusion, though I am wary of blame Kipnis places on Title IX policy.

6. Joseph J. Fischel takes up this and other complications of consent in *Sex and Harm in the Age of Consent* (2016).

7. Doyle's insightful blog post "Notes on Anti-Harassment Writing" (2017) further reflects on the institutional ecology of harassment and the ethical problems of writing about it.

8. In her *Signs* interview, MacKinnon (2018) reflects on the limits of the law as a tool, and on cultural changes made outside of it: "Many of the most notable actions coming out of #MeToo are things that the law isn't set up to do. The legal claim for sexual harassment as a civil right is focused on getting relief for the person abused. It doesn't even permit, as a strict legal consequence, doing anything to the perpetrator. So what is most remarkable about the present moment is seeing women coming forward and saying what various quite powerful men have done to them and watching other powerful men come to the very swift conclusion—this is what is new here—that they can't afford to keep these men around or be associated with them or their work product. Their former conclusion was that they didn't want the women around. That is the big reversal of the present time."

Chapter 3. Racial (In)Sensitivity

1. TheDemands.org was run by Black Liberation Collective, a "fiscally sponsored project of Netroots Foundation" (see https://web.archive.org/web/20220616150932/http://www.blackliberationcollective.org/about-1).

2. Here I follow the "rhetorical deployment of the term *murder*" outlined in Ore 2019, author's note.

3. McElderry and Rivera offer an on-the-ground perspective that I think is useful for getting the full context of events on campus; for a broader account focused on misinformation about the protests, see Vivian, *Campus Misinformation*, 41–47.

4. For a reflection on the hunger strike as a student activist tactic, see Nyong'o (2015); for more on hunger and resistance, see P. Anderson (2010) (cited in Nyong'o 2015).

5. See Thomason (2015) on the racist threats at Mizzou posted on the anonymous social media app Yik Yak.

6. While I was composing this chapter, students at the prestigious historically Black Howard University concluded a monthlong campout protest of poor housing conditions on the campus (N. Ellis 2021), demonstrating that the health and safety of students' living space on campus is an integral condition for learning.

7. For more on the tension of this exposure, see Williams (2019).

8. Blaming feminists for students' sensitivity is also a common rhetorical tactic in critiques of trigger warnings; see chapter 1.

9. There is certainly an evolution to be traced from the commonplaces against critical race theory in circulation in this piece from 2015 to President Trump's 2020 directive to end any federally funded racial sensitivity trainings drawing on critical race theory (Schwartz 2020), and the subsequent and ongoing attacks on critical race theory mounted by state legislatures.

10. In 2020, the Special Committee on Composing a CCCC Statement on Anti-Black Racism and Black Linguistic Justice, Or, Why We Cain't Breathe! issued "This Ain't Another Statement! This is a DEMAND for Black Linguistic Justice!" which directs the language of the demand toward the transformation of the profession and professional organization (https://cccc.ncte.org/cccc/demand-for-black-linguistic-justice).

11. For an explication of the lineage I draw on with this term, see Gerdes (2014).

12. Cole (2020) suggests that the action of university presidents can be instrumental on issues of racial justice in higher education.

Chapter 4. Vulnerability to Violence

1. During the debate that preceded the law's passage, I was a PhD candidate at the University of Texas at Austin. By the time the law was implemented, I had graduated and moved to Lubbock, Texas, to join the faculty at Texas Tech University. I've since joined the faculty at the University of Utah, which lost its own battle with the state legislature in 2004 when Utah became the first state in the United States to allow campus carry.

2. This history excludes laws pertaining to K–12 campuses, where firearms are prohibited by both state and federal law, with some exceptions (see Texas Association of School Boards Legal Services 2022). The touchstone for K–12 gun policy in Texas is (or ought to be) the shooting at Robb Elementary School in Uvalde, Texas, on May 24, 2022. The spectacular failures of multiple law enforcement agency responders and of multiple levels of public policy are the subjects of ongoing debate, if not deliberation.

3. Only 22% of students support campus carry, if the results of a study of midwestern colleges hold in other regional contexts (Thompson, Price, and Dake et al. 2013); for more recent and Texas-specific data, see Ruoppila and Butters (2021, 6), in which 71% of surveyed undergraduates at UT Austin opposed the policy, and 24% supported it (5% had no opinion).

4. For more on race and catachresis, see Calvin Warren's *Ontological Terror: Blackness, Nihilism, and Emancipation* (2018).

5. Psychoanalyst JoAnn Ponder (2018), who enrolled as a freshman at UT in 1972, reviews a variety of arguments surrounding the presence of a brain tumor compressing Whitman's amygdala that was discovered in his autopsy. Ponder, following the 1966 governor's report, contends that "the safest conclusion" is that "the tumor contributed to [Whitman's] problems, but was not the sole cause of his behavior" (242). Kristeen Cherney and Margaret Price (2018) remind us that while stigma about mental health and disability often increases in response to mass shootings, there is no consistent mental health profile that could be used to prevent acts of violence (103,

106). They also point out that people with mental health disabilities are far more likely to be victims of violence than its perpetrators (106).

6. I have not listed this work in my references because it was quickly discredited after its publication. For more on the author's manipulation of data to support his thesis, see Ludwig 1998 and Hemenway 1998.

7. See chapter 1, note 6. Stupidity implicates knowledge, Ronell contends, because it "knows that it does not know" (2002, 118).

8. See Eberly (2018), chapter 2.

9. Although it serves as a focal point for this chapter, the violence on UT's campus is not exceptional. Some incidences attract a large national media spotlight, like the 2018 murder of University of Utah student Lauren McCluskey; other cases, like the 2022 murder of University of Utah student Zhifan Dong, are marginalized. Although college campuses are generally regarded as safer than many of the cities that are home to them, the National Center for Education Statistics (2021b) reported 28,506 crimes against "persons and property" on college campuses in their most recent year, 2018.

Reference List

7 Humanities Professors. 2014. "Trigger Warnings Are Flawed." *Inside Higher Ed*, May 29. www.insidehighered.com/views/2014/05/29/essay-faculty-members-about-why-they-will-not-use-trigger-warnings.

Ahmad, Muhammad. 1978. "On the Black Student Movement—1960–70." In "The 1960's," special issue, *Black Scholar* 9, no. 8/9 (May/June): 2–11.

Ahmed, Sara. 2012. *On Being Included: Racism and Diversity in Institutional Life*. Durham, NC: Duke University Press.

Ahmed, Sara. 2015. "Against Students." *Feminist Killjoys*, June 25. feminist-killjoys.com/2015/06/25/against-students.

Ahmed, Sara. 2016. "Interview with Judith Butler." *Sexualities* 19 (4): 482–92.

Ahmed, Sara. 2017. *Living a Feminist Life*. Durham, NC: Duke University Press.

Ahmed, Sara. 2021. *Complaint!* Durham, NC: Duke University Press.

Alcorn, Marshall W. 2002. *Changing the Subject in English Class: Discourse and the Constructions of Desire*. Carbondale: Southern Illinois University Press.

Alden, Andrea, Kendall Gerdes, Judy Holiday, and Ryan Skinnell. 2019. "Introduction: Methodically Re/Membering Theory—Crowleyan Inventions." In *Reinventing (with) Theory in Rhetoric and Writing Studies: Essays in Honor of Sharon Crowley*, 3–15. Louisville, CO: University Press of Colorado/Utah State University Press.

Alexander, Jonathan, Susan C. Jarratt, and Nancy Welch. 2018. "Introduction." *Unruly Rhetorics: Protest, Persuasion, and Publics*. Pittsburgh, PA: University of Pittsburgh Press.

Allen, Ira J. 2018. *The Ethical Fantasy of Rhetorical Theory*. Pittsburgh, PA: University of Pittsburgh Press.

Anderson, Elizabeth. 2006. "Recent Thinking about Sexual Harassment: A Review Essay." *Philosophy and Public Affairs* 34 (3): 284–312.

Anderson, Patrick. 2010. *So Much Wasted: Hunger, Performance, and the Morbidity of Resistance.* Durham, NC: Duke University Press.

Asen, Robert. 2015. *Democracy, Deliberation, and Education.* University Park: Pennsylvania State University Press.

Austin. J. L. 1962. *How to Do Things with Words.* Cambridge, MA: Harvard University Press.

Baer, Ulrich. 2017. "What 'Snowflakes' Get Right about Free Speech." *New York Times*, April 24. www.nytimes.com/2017/04/24/opinion/what-liberal-snowflakes-get-right-about-free-speech.html.

Baer, Ulrich. 2019. *What Snowflakes Get Right: Free Speech, Truth, and Equality on Campus.* New York: Oxford University Press.

Bailie, Brian. 2020. "So, Richard Spencer Is Coming to Your Campus. How He Was Allowed On, and How You Can Confront Him." *Present Tense: A Journal of Rhetoric in Society* 8, no. 2 (July 15): http://www.presenttensejournal.org/volume-8/so-richard-spencer-is-coming-to-your-campus-how-he-was-allowed-on-and-how-you-can-confront-him/.

Balthaser, Benjamin (@BL_Balthaser). 2022. "It's not surprising that after decades of defunding/privatization, I hear not only on the right but on the left a growing hostility to 'the university' as a social institution . . . ," Twitter, thread, September 11. https://twitter.com/BL_Balthaser/status/1569085747763838978.

Barnard, Ian. 2020. *Sex Panic Rhetorics: Queer Interventions.* Tuscaloosa: University of Alabama Press.

Barnes, Aurora Temple. 2017. "Guns and Academic Freedom." *Gonzaga Law Review* 53:1–42. Preprint, March 14.

Barthélemy, Hélène. 2020. "How Men's Rights Groups Helped Rewrite Regulations on Campus Rape." *Nation*, August 14. https://www.thenation.com/article/politics/betsy-devos-title-ix-mens-rights.

Bartholomae, David. 1986. "Inventing the University." *Journal of Basic Writing* 5 (1): 4–23.

Bass, Scott A., and Mary L. Clark. 2015. "The Gravest Threat to Colleges Comes from Within." *Chronicle of Higher Education*, September 28. http://chronicle.com/article/The-Gravest-Threat-to-Colleges/233449.

Bates, Karen Grigsby. 2015. "Hands Up Don't Shoot: Thoughts from the Mizzou Photog Blocked during Protest." *NPR Code Switch: Race and Identity, Remixed.* November 13. https://www.npr.org/sections/codeswitch/2015/11/13/455919183/hands-up-dont-shoot-mizzou-students-block-photog-during-protest.

Bedera, Nicole. 2021. "Beyond Trigger Warnings: A Survivor-Centered

Approach to Teaching on Sexual Violence and Avoiding Institutional Betrayal." *Teaching Sociology* 49 (3): 267–77.

Bejan, Teresa M. 2017. "The Two Clashing Meanings of 'Free Speech.'" *Atlantic*, December 2. https://www.theatlantic.com/politics/archive/2017/12/two-concepts-of-freedom-of-speech/546791/.

Ben-Porath, Sigal R. 2017. *Free Speech on Campus*. Philadelphia: University of Pennsylvania Press.

Berrett, Dan. 2015. "Stunned by a Video, University of Oklahoma Struggles to Talk about Race." *Chronicle of Higher Education*, March 19. http://www.chronicle.com/article/Stunned-by-a-Video-U-of/228611.

Bérubé, Michael, and Jennifer Ruth. 2015. *The Humanities, Higher Education, and Academic Freedom: Three Necessary Arguments*. New York: Palgrave Macmillan.

Bérubé, Michael, and Jennifer Ruth. 2022. *It's Not Free Speech: Race, Democracy, and the Future of Academic Freedom*. Baltimore, MD: Johns Hopkins University Press.

Biondi, Martha. 2012. *The Black Revolution on Campus*. Berkeley: University of California Press.

Bishop, Wendy. 1993. "Writing Is/and Therapy? Raising Questions about Writing Classrooms and Writing Program Administration." *Journal of Advanced Composition* 13 (2): 503–516.

Boedy, Matthew. 2020. *May 1970*. Lexington, KY: Intermezzo. https://manifold.as.uky.edu/projects/may-1970-boedy.

Boedy, Matthew. 2022. "Ten Years of Turning Point USA: From Free Markets to Freedom Square." *Political Research Associates*, January 28. https://politicalresearch.org/2022/01/28/ten-years-turning-point-usa.

Boggioni, Tom. 2015. "Armed Vet Destroys Gun Nuts' Argument on Mass Shooters by Explaining Why He Didn't Attack Oregon Killer." *RawStory*, October 2. https://www.rawstory.com/2015/10/armed-vet-destroys-gun-nuts-argument-on-mass-shooters-by-explaining-why-he-didnt-attack-oregon-killer/.

Boland, Mary R. 2007. "The Stakes of Not Staking Our Claim: Academic Freedom and the Subject of Composition." *College English* 70 (1): 32–51.

Boler, Megan. 2006. *Democratic Dialogue in Education: Troubling Speech, Disturbing Silence*. Lausanne, Switzerland: Peter Lang.

boyd, danah. 2018. "Media Manipulation, Strategic Amplification, and Responsible Journalism." *Points*, Data & Society Research Institute. September 14. https://points.datasociety.net/media-manipulation-strategic-amplification-and-responsible-journalism-95f4d611f462.

Boyle, Casey. 2018. "The Complete History of Parlin Hall (Abridged Version)." In *Inventing Place: Writing Lone Star Rhetorics*, edited by Casey

Boyle and Jenny Rice, 59–72. Carbondale: Southern Illinois University Press.

Braceras, Jennifer C. 2017. "'Sexual Paranoia Comes to Campus.'" *National Review*, April 6. https://www.nationalreview.com/2017/04/laura-kipnis -title-ix-academic-freedom-unwanted-advances-chronicle-higher-educa tion-wellesley-college/.

Bradley, Ariella C. 2017. "As Much as Things Change, They Stay the Same: How the Campus Administration Responds to Black Students' Concerns about Climate." Master's thesis, California State University, Long Beach.

Brief for the AAUP as Amicus Curiae. 2017. *Glass et al. v. Paxton et al.* United States Court of Appeals for the Fifth Circuit. https://www.aaup.org/ file/Glass_campus_carry_0.pdf.

Britzky, Haley. 2019. "Young Military Hopefuls Are Willing to Go to War for Their Country. Instead, Many Are Losing Their Lives in School Shootings." *Business Insider*, https://www.businessinsider.com/young-us -military-prospects-dying-in-school-shootings-instead-2019-5.

Brown, James J., Jr. 2015. *Hospitality and the Rhetorics of Software*. Ann Arbor: University of Michigan Digital Culture Books.

Brown, Sarah. 2015. "At Yale, Painful Rifts Emerge over Diversity and Free Speech." *Chronicle of Higher Education*, November 9. http://www.chron icle.com/article/At-Yale-Painful-Rifts-Emerge/234112.

Brown, Sarah, and Katherine Mangan. 2018. "What You Need to Know about the Proposed Title IX Regulations." *Chronicle of Higher Education*, November 16. https://www.chronicle.com/article/What-You-Need-to -Know-About/245118.

Bugeja, Michael. 2021. "Updating the Trigger Warning in Contentious Times." *Inside Higher Ed*. August 25. https://www.insidehighered.com/ views/2021/08/25/why-trigger-warnings-are-needed-now-much-more -ever-opinion.

Burke, Kenneth. (1950) 1969. *A Rhetoric of Motives*. Oakland: University of California Press.

Burr, Beverly. 1988. "History of Student Activism at the University of Texas at Austin (1960–1988)." Undergraduate thesis, University of Texas at Austin.

Burrows, Cedric D. 2020. *Rhetorical Crossover: The Black Presence in White Culture*. Pittsburgh, PA: University of Pittsburgh Press.

Butler, Judith. 1997. *Excitable Speech: A Politics of the Performative*. Oxford-shire, UK: Routledge.

Butler, Judith. (2004) 2006. *Precarious Life: The Powers of Mourning and Violence*. New York: Verso.

Butler, Judith. 2005. *Giving an Account of Oneself.* New York: Fordham University Press.

Butler, Judith. 2006. "Academic Norms, Contemporary Challenges: A Reply to Robert Post on Academic Freedom." In *Academic Freedom after September 11,* edited by Beshara Doumani, 107–142. New York: Zone Books.

Butler, Judith. 2013. "Academic Freedom and the ASA's Boycott of Israel: A Response to Michelle Goldberg." *Nation,* December 8. https://www.thenation.com/article/archive/academic-freedom-and-asas-boycott-israel-response-michelle-goldberg/.

Butler, Judith. 2015. "Exercising Rights: Academic Freedom and Boycott Politics." In *Who's Afraid of Academic Freedom?,* edited by Akeel Bilgrami and Jonathan Cole, 293–315. New York: Columbia University Press.

Buzuvis, Erin. 2017. "Title IX and Procedural Fairness: Why Disciplined Student Litigation Does Not Undermine the Role of Title IX in Campus Sexual Assault." *Montana Law Review* 78 (1): 71–108.

Byrne, Peter J. 1989. "Academic Freedom: A 'Special Concern of the First Amendment.'" *Yale Law Journal* 99, no. 2 (November): 251–340.

Calafell, Bernadette Marie, and Ersula Ore. 2021. "A Conversation on Activism, Solidarity, and Burnout in the Academy." *Rhetoric and Public Affairs* 24, no. 1–2: 129–48.

Cantor, David, Bonnie Fisher, Susan Chiball, Reanne Townsend, Hyunshik Lee, Carol Bruce, and Gail Thomas. 2017. "Report on the AAU Campus Climate Survey on Sexual Assault and Sexual Misconduct." *Association of American Universities,* October 20. https://www.nsvrc.org/sites/default/files/2021-04/aau-report_rev-01-17-2020.pdf.

Carter, Angela. 2015. "Teaching with Trauma: Trigger Warnings, Feminism, and Disability Pedagogy." *Disability Studies Quarterly* 35, no. 2. dsq-sds.org/article/view/4652/3935.

Carter, TaLisa J., and Miltonette O. Craig. 2022. "It Could Be Us: Black Faculty as 'Threats' on the Path to Tenure." *Race and Justice* 12 (3): 569–87.

Caruth, Cathy. 1996. *Unclaimed Experience: Trauma, Narrative, and History.* Baltimore, MD: Johns Hopkins University Press.

Chávez, Karma R. 2013. *Queer Migration Politics: Activist Rhetoric and Coalitional Possibilities.* Champaign: University of Illinois Press.

Cherney, Kristeen, and Margaret Price. 2018. "Student Profiling and Negative Implications for Students with Disabilities." In *The Wiley Handbook on Violence in Education: Forms, Factors, and Preventions,* edited by Harvey Shapiro, 103–117. New York: Wiley.

Chessman, Hollie, and Lindsay Wayt. 2016. "What Are Students Demanding?" *Higher Education Today*, American Council on Education. January 13. https://www.higheredtoday.org/2016/01/13/what-are-students-de manding/.

Chu, Simone C., and Iris M. Lewis. 2019. "What Happens Next with Title IX: DeVos's Proposed Rule, Explained." *Harvard Crimson*, February 27. https://www.thecrimson.com/article/2019/2/27/title-ix-explainer/.

Cloud, Dana L. 2015. "'Civility' as a Threat to Academic Freedom." *First Amendment Studies* 49 (1): 13–17.

Cloud, Dana L. 2017. "Responding to Right-Wing Attacks." *Inside Higher Ed*, November 7. https://www.insidehighered.com/advice/2017/11/07/ tips-help-academics-respond-right-wing-attacks-essay.

Cokley, Kevin. 2016. "IUPRA Poll Results: Texas Voters' Attitudes about Gun Laws." *Institute for Urban Policy Research and Analysis*, April 26.

Cole, Eddie R. 2020. *The Campus Color Line: College Presidents and the Struggle for Black Freedom*. Princeton, NJ: Princeton University Press.

Cole, Jonathan, Stephen Cole, and Christopher C. Weiss. 2015. "Academic Freedom: A Pilot Study of Faculty Views." In *Who's Afraid of Academic Freedom*, edited by Akeel Bilgrami and Jonathan Cole, 343–94. New York: Columbia University Press.

Committee A. 2014. *On Trigger Warnings*. American Association of University Professors, August. https://www.aaup.org/file/2014-Trigger_ Warnings.pdf.

Concerned Student 1950. 2015. *List of Demands*. October 20. https://www .columbiamissourian.com/demands-of-concerned-student-1950/pdf_ a80bc06e-784a-11e5-a620-2b2cb43219fe.html.

Corrigan, Lisa M. 2016. "On Rhetorical Criticism, Performativity, and White Fragility." *Review of Communication* 16 (1): 86–88.

Cottom, Daniel. 1981. "Taste and the Civilized Imagination." *Journal of Aesthetics and Art Criticism* 39 (4): 367–80.

Couch, Todd. 2014. "'Arming the Good Guys?' An Examination of Racial Framing in Students for Concealed Carry on Campus." PhD diss., Texas A&M University.

Crowley, Sharon. 1995. "Biting the Hand That Feeds Us: Nineteenth-Century Uses of a Pedagogy of Taste." In *Rhetoric, Cultural Studies, and Literacy: Selected Papers from the 1994 Conference of the Rhetoric Society of America*, edited by John Frederick Reynolds, 11–20. Hillsdale, NJ: Lawrence Erlbaum Associates.

Crowley, Sharon. 1998. *Composition in the University: Historical and Polemical Essays*. Pittsburgh, PA: University of Pittsburgh Press.

Crowley, Sharon. 2006. *Toward a Civil Discourse: Rhetoric and Fundamentalism*. Pittsburgh, PA: University of Pittsburgh Press.

Cryer, Daniel A. 2020. "The Good Man Shooting Well: Authoritarian Submission and Aggression in the 'Gun-Citizen.'" *Rhetoric Society Quarterly* 50 (4): 254–67.

Cvetkovich, Ann. 2012. *Depression: A Public Feeling*. Durham, NC: Duke University Press.

Czajka, Kelley. 2019. "As the Comment Period for Proposed Title IX Changes Ends, Nearly 100,000 Have Weighed In." *Pacific Standard*, January 30. https://psmag.com/news/as-the-comment-period-for-proposed -title-ix-changes-ends-nearly-100000-have-weighed-in.

Daily Texan Editorial Board. 2013. "Regents, Powers and Lege Repeat History When They Fight." *Daily Texan*, April 1. https://thedailytexan .com/2013/04/01/regents-powers-lege-repeat-history-when-they-fight/.

Dart, Tom. 2016. "Cocks Not Glocks: Texas Students Carry Dildos on Campus to Protest Gun Law." *Guardian*, August 25. https://www .theguardian.com/us-news/2016/aug/25/cocks-not-glocks-texas-cam pus-carry-gun-law-protest.

Davis, Diane. 2000. "Confessions of an Anacoluthon: Avital Ronell on Writing, Technology, Pedagogy, Politics." *JAC* 20 (2): 243–281.

Davis, Diane. 2010. *Inessential Solidarity: Rhetoric and Foreigner Relations*. Pittsburgh, PA: University of Pittsburgh Press.

DeChavez, Yvette. 2018. "It's Time to Decolonize That Syllabus." *Los Angeles Times*, October 8. https://www.latimes.com/books/la-et-jc-decolo nize-syllabus-20181008-story.html.

Derrida, Jacques. (1997) 2000. *Of Hospitality*. Translated by Rachel Bowlby. Redwood City, CA: Stanford University Press.

Derrida, Jacques. (2006) 2008. *The Animal That Therefore I Am*. Translated by David Wills. New York: Fordham University Press.

Detweiler, Eric. 2022. *Responsible Pedagogy: Moving beyond Authority and Mastery in Higher Education*. University Park: Pennsylvania State University Press.

Donnelly, Michael. 2016. *Freedom of Speech and the Function of Rhetoric in the United States*. Lanham, MD: Lexington Books.

Doyle, Jennifer. 2015. *Campus Sex, Campus Security*. South Pasadena, CA: Semiotext(e).

Doyle, Jennifer. 2017. "Notes on Anti-harassment Writing." *Trouble Thinking*. July 1, https://troublethinking.com/2017/07/01/notes-on-anti-ha rassment-writing/.

Drum, Kevin. 2014. "What's the End Game for the Trigger Warning Movement?" *Mother Jones*, May 19. www.motherjones.com/kevin-drum/20 14/05/whats-end-game-trigger-warning-movement.

Duggan, Lisa. 2014. "On Trauma and Trigger Warnings, in Three Parts."

Bully Bloggers. November 23. bullybloggers.wordpress.com/2014/11/23/on-trauma-and-trigger-warnings-in-three-parts.

Eatman, Megan. 2020. *Ecologies of Harm: Rhetorics of Violence in the United States.* Columbus: Ohio State University Press.

Eberly, Rosa A. 2000. *Citizen Critics: Literary Public Spheres.* Champaign: University of Illinois Press.

Eberly, Rosa A. 2004. "'Everywhere You Go, It's There': Forgetting and Remembering the University of Texas Tower Shootings." In *Framing Public Memory*, edited by Kendall Phillips, 65–88. Tuscaloosa: University of Alabama Press.

Eberly, Rosa A. 2016. "Texas Picked an Ominous Date to Arm Its Public Colleges." *Chronicle of Higher Education*, July 27. https://www.chronicle.com/article/Texas-Picked-an-Ominous-Date/237264.

Eberly, Rosa A. 2018. *Towers of Rhetoric: Memory and Reinvention.* Intermezzo. http://intermezzo.enculturation.net/05-eberly/eberly-tor-title.html.

Edelman, KJ. 2019. "White Supremacist Manifesto Allegedly AirDropped to Students, DPS Says." *Daily Orange*, November 19. http://dailyorange.com/2019/11/white-supremacist-manifesto-allegedly-airdropped-students-dps-says/.

Edman, Jeanne L., Susan B. Watson, and David J. Patron. 2015. "Trauma and Psychological Distress among Ethnically Diverse Community College Students." *Community College Journal of Research and Practice* 40 (4): 335–42.

Elder, Cristyn L., and Bethany Davila. 2019. *Defining, Locating, and Addressing Bullying in the WPA Workplace.* Louisville, CO: University Press of Colorado/Utah State University Press.

Ellis, Lindsay. 2017. "Posters at UT Latest Display of Campus Post-election Racism." *Houston Chronicle*, February 14. https://www.chron.com/local/education/campus-chronicles/article/Racist-posters-at-UT-latest-post-election-10931366.php.

Ellis, Nicquel Terry. 2021. "Howard Students Reach Agreement with University Officials after Month-Long Protest over Poor Housing Conditions." *CNN*, November 15. https://www.cnn.com/2021/11/15/us/howard-protests-housing-agreement-reached/index.html.

Esch, Elizabeth, Megan Jones, and David Roediger. 2018. "Academic Freedom under the Gun: A Report from Kansas." *AAUP Journal of Academic Freedom* 9:1–11.

Espinosa, Lorelle, Hollie Chessman, and Lindsay Wayt. 2016. "Racial Climate on Campus: A Survey of College Presidents." *Higher Education Today*, American Council on Education, March 8. http://www.higheredtoday.org/2016/03/08/racial-climate-on-campus-a-survey-of-college-presidents/.

Evans, Sara. (1979) 1980. *Personal Politics: The Roots of Women's Liberation in the Civil Rights Movement and the New Left*. New York: Random House, Vintage Books Edition.

Feagin, Joe R., and Melvin P. Sikes. 1995. "How Black Students Cope with Racism on White Campuses." *Journal of Blacks in Higher Education* 8:91–97.

Felman, Shoshana. 1982. "Psychoanalysis and Education: Teaching Terminable and Interminable." In "The Pedagogical Imperative: Teaching as a Literary Genre," special issue, *Yale French Studies* no. 63: 21–44.

Ferguson, Roderick A. 2012. *The Reorder of Things: The University and Its Pedagogies of Minority Difference*. Minneapolis: University of Minnesota Press.

Ferguson, Roderick A. 2017. *We Demand: The University and Student Protests*. Oakland: University of California Press.

Fernandez, Lourdes, Heidi Y. Lawrence, and Bonnie Stabile. 2020. "The Disappearing Accused: Rhetoric, Narrative, and Campus Sexual Assault." *Rhetoric Review* 39 (2): 230–45.

Ferré-Sadurní, Luis. 2019. "Syracuse University Suspends Fraternity Activities after Racist Incident." *New York Times*, November 17. https://www.nytimes.com/2019/11/17/nyregion/racist-fraternity-syracuse-university.html.

Filipovic, Jill. 2014. "We've Gone Too Far with 'Trigger Warnings.'" *Guardian*, March 5. www.theguardian.com/commentisfree/2014/mar/05/trigger-warnings-can-be-counterproductive.

Fischel, Joseph J. 2016. *Sex and Harm in the Age of Consent*. Minneapolis: University of Minnesota Press.

Fish, Stanley. 2014. *Versions of Academic Freedom: From Professionalism to the Revolution*. Chicago: University of Chicago Press.

Flaherty, Colleen. 2014. "Trigger Unhappy." *Inside Higher Ed*, April 14. www.insidehighered.com/news/2014/04/14/oberlin-backs-down-trigger-warnings-professors-who-teach-sensitive-material.

Flaherty, Colleen. 2017a. "A Hill to Retire On?" *Inside Higher Ed*, September 15. www.insidehighered.com/news/2017/09/15/atmospheric-scientist-illinois-leave-after-refusing-provide-lecture-slides-student.

Flaherty, Colleen. 2017b. "AAUP Files Brief in Challenge to Campus Carry." *Insider Higher Ed*, November 22. https://www.insidehighered.com/quicktakes/2017/11/22/aaup-files-brief-challenge-campus-carry.

Folts, Emma. 2019. "Syverud Agrees to Meet Protestors' Demands." *Daily Orange*, November 21. http://dailyorange.com/2019/11/syverud-agrees-meet-protesters-demands/.

Foss, Sonja K., and Cindy L. Griffin. 1995. "Beyond Persuasion: A Proposal for an Invitational Rhetoric." *Communication Monographs* 62 (1): 2–18.

Fox, Catherine. 2007. "From Transaction to Transformation: (En)Countering White Heteronormativity in 'Safe Spaces.'" *College English* 69 (5): 496–511.

Frank, Thomas. 2014. "The Trigger Warning We Need: 'College is a Scam Meant to Perpetuate the 1 Percent.'" *Salon*, May 25. www.salon .com/2014/05/25/the_1_percents_college_scam.

Frazier, Patricia, Samantha Anders, and Sulani Perera. 2009. "Traumatic Events among Undergraduate Students: Prevalence and Associated Symptoms." *Journal of Counseling Psychology* 56 (3): 450–60.

Friedersdorf, Conor. 2015. "Campus Activists Weaponize 'Safe Space.'" *Atlantic*, November 10. https://www.theatlantic.com/politics/archive /2015/11/how-campus-activists-are-weaponizing-the-safe-space/415 080/.

Friedman, Matthew. 2012. *Posttraumatic and Acute Stress Disorders*. New York: Springer.

Gajda, Amy. 2009. *The Trials of Academe: The New Era of Campus Litigation*. Cambridge, MA: Harvard University Press.

Gallop, Jane. 1997. *Feminist Accused of Sexual Harassment*. Durham, NC: Duke University Press.

General Body. 2019. "Letter to the Editor: THE General Body Members Support Resignation of Chancellor." *Daily Orange*, November 19. http:// dailyorange.com/2019/11/letters-to-the-editor-the-general-body-mem bers-support-resignation-of-chancellor/.

Gerdes, Kendall. 2014. "Performativity." In "Postposttranssexual: Key Concepts for a 21st Century Transgender Studies," edited by Susan Stryker and Paisley Currah, special issue, *Transgender Studies Quarterly* 1, nos. 1/2 (Spring): 148–50. http://tsq.dukejournals.org/content/1/1-2/148. full.

Gerdes, Kendall. 2019a. "Rhetorical Futurity, or Desiring Theory." In *Reinventing (with) Theory in Rhetoric and Writing Studies: Essays in Honor of Sharon Crowley*, edited by Andrea Alden, Kendall Gerdes, Judy Holiday, and Ryan Skinnell, 231–42. Louisville, CO: University Press of Colorado/Utah State University Press.

Gerdes, Kendall. 2019b. "Trauma, Trigger Warnings, and the Rhetoric of Sensitivity." *Rhetoric Society Quarterly* 49 (1): 3–24.

Gersen, Jacob, and Jeannie Suk. 2016. "The Sex Bureaucracy." *California Law Review* 104: 880–948.

Gersen, Jeannie Suk. 2021. "What If Trigger Warnings Don't Work?" *New Yorker*, September 28. https://www.newyorker.com/news/our-colum nists/what-if-trigger-warnings-dont-work.

Gertner, Nancy. 2015. "Sex, Lies, and Justice." *American Prospect*, January 12. https://prospect.org/justice/sex-lies-justice/.

Giroux, Susan Searls. 2000. "Race, Rhetoric, and the Contest over Civic Education." *JAC* 20 (2): 311–48.

Glass et al. v. Paxton et al. 2016. United States District Court for the Western District of Texas Austin Division. No. 1:16-cv-845.

Goggin, Peter N., and Maureen Daly Goggin. 2005. "Presence in Absence: Discourses and Teaching (in, on, and about) Trauma." In *Trauma and the Teaching of Writing*, edited by Shane Borrowman, 29–52. Albany: State University of New York Press.

Goldberg, Beverly. 2010. "UT Austin Shooting Rampage Ends Tragically in the Library." *American Libraries Magazine*, September 28. https://americanlibrariesmagazine.org/2010/09/28/ut-austin-shooting-rampage-ends-tragically-in-the-library/.

Goldberg, Jonah. 2014. "The Peculiar Madness of 'Trigger Warnings.'" *Los Angeles Times*, March 19. www.latimes.com/opinion/op-ed/la-oe-goldberg-trigger-warnings-20140520-column.html.

Gorgias. (1972) 2001. "Encomium of Helen." In *The Older Sophists*, translated by George Kennedy, edited by Rosamond Kent Sprague, 50–54. Columbia: University of South Carolina Press.

Grayson, Mara Lee. 2020. *Race Talk in the Age of the Trigger Warning: Recognizing and Challenging Classroom Cultures of Silence.* Lanham, MD: Rowman and Littlefield.

Green, Erica L. 2018. "New US Sexual Misconduct Rules Bolster Rights of Accused and Protect Colleges." *New York Times*, August 29. https://www.nytimes.com/2018/08/29/us/politics/devos-campus-sexual-assault.html.

Greenberg, Zoe. 2018. "What Happens to #MeToo When a Feminist Is the Accused?" *New York Times*, August 13. https://www.nytimes.com/2018/08/13/nyregion/sexual-harassment-nyu-female-professor.html.

Group of Concerned and Unapologetic Students of Color. 2015. "An Open Letter to the Wesleyan Community from Students of Color." *Wesleying*, September 25. http://wesleying.org/2015/09/25/an-open-letter-to-the-wesleyan-community-from-students-of-color/.

Gusa, Diane Lynn. 2010. "White Institutional Presence: The Impact of Whiteness on Campus Climate." *Harvard Educational Review* 80 (4): 464–89.

Halberstam, Jack. 2014. "You Are Triggering Me! The Neoliberal Rhetoric of Harm, Danger and Trauma." *Bully Bloggers*, July 5. bullybloggers.wordpress.com/2014/07/05/you-are-triggering-me-the-neo-liberal-rhetoric-of-harm-danger-and-trauma.

Halberstam, Jack. 2017. "Trigger Happy: From Content Warning to Censorship." *Signs: Journal of Women in Culture and Society* 42 (2): 535–42.

Hall, Katie. 2016. "UT Professors: 3 Bullet Casings, One with Note Inside, Left on Campus." *Austin American-Statesman*, September 20. https://www.statesman.com/story/news/2016/09/20/ut-professors-3-bullet-casings-one-with-note-inside-left-on-campus/9949774007/.

Halley, Janet. 2015. "Trading the Megaphone for the Gavel in Title IX Enforcement." *Harvard Law Review Forum* 128: 103–17.

Handa, Sahil. 2019. "What Conservatives Get Wrong about the Campus Wars." *National Review*, July 4. https://www.nationalreview.com/2019/07/what-conservatives-get-wrong-about-campus-wars-woke-culture/.

Hanlon, Aaron. 2015. "The Trigger Warning Myth." *New Republic*, August 14. https://newrepublic.com/article/122543/trigger-warning-myth.

Hanlon, Aaron. 2017. "Why Colleges Have a Right to Reject Hateful Speakers Like Ann Coulter." *New Republic*, April 24. https://newrepublic.com/article/142218/colleges-right-reject-hateful-speakers-like-ann-coulter.

Hatch, Justin D. 2019. "Dissociating Power and Racism: Stokely Carmichael at Berkeley." *Advances in the History of Rhetoric* 22 (3): 303–25.

"Hate's Insidious Face: UW-Milwaukee and the 'Alt-Right.'" 2016. *Overpass Light Brigade*, December 14. overpasslightbrigade.org/hates-insidious-face-uw-milwaukee-and-the-alt-right.

Hatemi, Pete. 2021. "What Do You Do When Hate Knocks on Your Door?" *Medium*, February 10. https://phatemi.medium.com/what-do-you-do-when-hate-knocks-on-your-door-2cfb99da7aed.

Hatewatch Staff. 2017. "Post-Election Bias Incidents up to 1,372; New Collaboration with ProPublica." *Southern Poverty Law Center*. February 10. https://www.splcenter.org/hatewatch/2017/02/10/post-election-bias-incidents-1372-new-collaboration-propublica.

Hemenway, David. 1998. "Review." *New England Journal of Medicine* 339 (27): 2029–30.

Herman, Judith. 1992. *Trauma and Recovery: The Aftermath of Violence—From Domestic Abuse to Political Terror*. New York: Basic Books.

Herzog, Karen. 2016. "GOP, UW at Odds Over 'Whiteness' Course." *Milwaukee Journal Sentinel*, December 21. www.jsonline.com/story/news/education/2016/12/21/gop-lawmakers-demand-uw-madison-drop-problem-whiteness-course/95694610.

Hesford, Wendy. 1999. "Reading *Rape Stories*: Material Rhetoric and the Trauma of Representation." *College English* 62 (2): 192–221.

Hill, Annie, and Carole A. Stabile. 2021. "Rhetoric and Sexual Violence: A Conversation with Annie Hill and Carol A. Stabile." *Rhetoric and Public Affairs* 24, nos. 1–2: 149–68.

Hoang, Haivan V. 2015. *Writing against Racial Injury: The Politics of Asian*

American Student Rhetoric. Pittsburgh, PA: University of Pittsburgh Press.

Hofstadter, Richard, and Walter P. Metzger. 1955. *The Development of Academic Freedom in the United States*. New York: Columbia University Press.

Holley, Lynn C., and Sue Steiner. 2005. "Safe Space: Student Perspectives on Classroom Environment." *Journal of Social Work Education* 41 (1): 49–64.

Hotchkins, Bryan A. 2017. "Black Student Leaders Practicing Resistance in the Midst of Chaos: Applying Transgenerational Activist Knowledge to Navigate a Predominantly White Institution." In "When Voices Rise: Race, Resistance, and Campus Uprisings in the Information Age," special issue, *Journal of Negro Education* 86 (3): 269–82.

Hotckins, Bryan A., and T. Elon Dancy. 2017. "A House Is Not a Home: Black Students' Responses to Racism in University Residential Halls." *Journal of College and University Student Housing* 43 (3): 42–53.

Institute of Public Affairs. 1970. "The Sixty-First Texas Legislature: A Review of Its Work." University of Texas. https://lrl.texas.gov/scanned/sessionOverviews/review/61st.pdf.

Jackson, Rachel C. 2017. "Decolonizing Place and Race: Racial Resentments, Local Histories, and Transrhetorical Analysis." *Symposium: Race, Rhetoric, and Resentment in Rhetoric Review* 36 (4): 292–301.

Jarratt, Susan. 1991. "Feminism and Composition: The Case for Conflict." In *Contending with Words: Composition and Rhetoric in a Postmodern Age*, edited by Patricia Harkin and John Schilb, 105–23. New York: Modern Language Association of America.

Jarvie, Jenny. 2014. "Trigger Happy." *New Republic*, March 3. www.newrepublic.com/article/116842/trigger-warnings-have-spread-blogs-college-classes-thats-bad.

Jaschik, Scott. 2016. "U Chicago to Freshmen: Don't Expect Safe Spaces." *Inside Higher Ed*, August 25. https://www.insidehighered.com/news/2016/08/25/u-chicago-warns-incoming-students-not-expect-safe-spaces-or-trigger-warnings.

Jaschik, Scott. 2017. "'Unprecedented' White Supremacist Activity." *Inside Higher Ed*, March 7. https://www.insidehighered.com/news/2017/03/07/report-documents-white-supremacist-activity-campuses.

Johnson, Jenell. 2010. "The Skeleton on the Couch: The Eagleton Affair, Rhetorical Disability, and the Stigma of Mental Illness." *Rhetoric Society Quarterly* 40 (5): 459–78.

Jones, Hannah E., and Sean M. Horan. 2019. "Guns on Campus: Campus

Carry and Instructor–Student Communication." *Communication Education* 68 (4): 417–37.

Jones, Payton J., Benjamin W. Bellet, and Richard J. McNally. 2020. "Helping or Harming? The Effect of Trigger Warnings on Individuals with Trauma Histories." *Clinical Psychological Science* 8 (5): 905–17.

Jones, Veronica A., and Richard J. Reddick. 2017. "The Heterogeneity of Resistance: How Black Students Utilize Engagement and Activism to Challenge PWI Inequalities," in "When Voices Rise: Race, Resistance, and Campus Uprisings in the Information Age," special issue, *Journal of Negro Education* 86 (3): 204–19.

Joyce, Kathryn. 2017. "The Takedown of Title IX." *New York Times*, December 5. https://www.nytimes.com/2017/12/05/magazine/the-take down-of-title-ix.html.

Kafer, Alison. 2016. "Un/Safe Disclosures: Scenes of Disability and Trauma." *Journal of Literary and Cultural Disability Studies* 10 (1): 1–20.

Kamenetz, Anya. 2018. "Professors Are Targets in Online Culture Wars; Some Fight Back." *All Things Considered*, NPR, April 4. https://www .npr.org/sections/ed/2018/04/04/590928008/professor-harassment.

Kelderman, Eric. 2015. "Upheaval in Missouri Highlights Football Players' Power." *Chronicle of Higher Education*, November 10. https://www .chronicle.com/article/Upheaval-in-Missouri/234130/.

Kennedy, Kelly, Michael de Yoanna, and Sonner Kehrt. 2022. "They Are the Good Guys with Guns. After Another Mass Shooting, Veterans Want Change." *War Horse*, June 2. https://thewarhorse.org/military-veterans -advocate-gun-control-after-texas-shooting/.

Khalid, Amna, and Jeffrey Aaron Snyder. 2021. "The Data Is In—Trigger Warnings Don't Work." *Chronicle of Higher Education*, September 15. https://www.chronicle.com/article/the-data-is-in-trigger-warnings -dont-work.

Kingkade, Tyler. 2014. "Fewer Than One-Third of Campus Sexual Assault Cases Result in Expulsion." *Huffington Post*, September 29. https://www .huffingtonpost.com/2014/09/29/campus-sexual-assault_n_5888742 .html.

Kingkade, Tyler. 2015. "Despite Fears about Trigger Warnings, Survey Suggests Few Faculty Are Forced to Use Them." *Huffington Post*, June 23. www.huffingtonpost.com/2015/06/23/faculty-trigger-warnings-sur vey_n_7639376.html.

Kipnis, Laura. 2015a. "Sexual Paranoia Strikes Academe." *Chronicle of Higher Education*, February 27. chronicle.com/article/Sexual-Paranoia -Strikes/190351.

Kipnis, Laura. 2015b. "My Title IX Inquisition." *Chronicle of Higher Edu-

cation, May 29. https://www.chronicle.com/article/my-title-ix-inquisi
tion/.

Kipnis, Laura. 2017. *Unwanted Advances: Sexual Paranoia Comes to Campus.*
New York: Harper.

Klein, Rebecca. 2018. "Lawsuit Accuses Betsy DeVos and Her Deputies
of Being Motivated by Sexism." *Huffington Post*, October 31. https://
www.huffingtonpost.com/entry/betsy-devos-sexual-assault-lawsuit_
us_5bd9ff6ee4b01abe6a1ad4a9.

Krebs, Christopher, Christine Lindquist, Marcus Berzofsky, Bonnie Shook-
Sa, and Kimberly Peterson. 2016. *Campus Climate Survey Validation
Study: Final Technical Report.* Bureau of Justice Statistics Research and
Development Series 100, January. http://www.bjs.gov/content/pub/pdf/
ccsvsftr.pdf.

Krebs, Christopher, Christine Lindquist, Tara D. Warner, Bonnie S. Fisher,
and Sandra L. Martin. 2007. *The Campus Sexual Assault (CSA) Study.*
Report prepared for the National Institute of Justice, December.

Kreighbaum, Andrew. 2018. "Under DeVos, a Smaller Department of
Education." *Inside Higher Ed*, June 13. https://www.insidehighered
.com/news/2018/06/13/education-department-staff-down-13-percent
-trump-administration-began.

Kynard, Carmen. 2013. *Vernacular Insurrections: Race, Black Protest, and the
New Century in Composition-Literacies Studies.* Albany: State University
of New York Press.

Laguardia, Francesca, Venezia Michalsen, and Holly Rider-Milkovich.
2017. "Trigger Warnings: From Panic to Data." *Journal of Legal Education* 66 (4): 882–903.

Largey, Matt. 2018. "Appeals Court Blocks Bid to Revive UT-Austin Professors' Lawsuit over Campus Carry." *KUT*, August 16. https://www.kut
.org/post/appeals-court-blocks-bid-revive-ut-austin-professors-lawsuit
-over-campus-carry.

LaRotta, Alex. 2017. "The TSU Riot, 50 Years Later." *Houston Chronicle*,
May 16. https://www.houstonchronicle.com/local/gray-matters/article/
The-TSU-Riot-50-years-later-11149852.php.

Larson, Stephanie R. 2021. *What It Feels Like: Visceral Rhetoric and the Politics of Rape Culture.* University Park: Pennsylvania State University Press.

Leath, Seanna, and Tabbye Chavous. 2017. "'We Really Protested': The
Influence of Sociopolitical Beliefs, Political Self-Efficacy, and Campus
Racial Climate on Civic Engagement among Black College Students
Attending Predominantly White Institutions." In "When Voices Rise:
Race, Resistance, and Campus Uprisings in the Information Age," spe-
cial issue, *Journal of Negro Education* 86 (3): 220–37.

Lee, Philip. 2018. "Student Protests and Academic Freedom in an Age of #BlackLivesMatter." *Ohio State Law Journal* 79 (2): 223–78.

LeMesurier, Jennifer. 2019. "Searching for Unseen Metic Labor in the Pussyhat Project." *Peitho: Journal of the Coalition of Feminist Scholars in the History of Rhetoric and Composition* 22 (1): https://cfshrc.org/article/searching-for-unseen-metic-labor-in-the-pussyhat-project.

Levinas, Emmanuel. (1961) 1991. *Totality and Infinity: An Essay on Exteriority.* Translated by Alphonso Lingis. Pittsburgh: Duquesne University Press.

Lewis, Shaundra K., and Daniel Alejandro De Luna. 2016. "Symposium on Texas Gun Law and the Future: The Fatal Flaws in Texas's Campus Carry Law." *Thurgood Marshall Law Review* 41 (2): 135–50.

Livingston, Kathleen Ann. 2014. "On Rage, Shame, 'Realness,' and Accountability to Survivors." *Harlot of the Arts* no. 12: https://pdxscholar.library.pdx.edu/harlot/vol12/iss12/4/.

Logan, Ginnie, Brian A. Lightfoot, and Ana Contreras. 2017. "Black and Brown Millennial Activism on a PWI Campus in the Era of Trump." In "When Voices Rise: Race, Resistance, and Campus Uprisings in the Information Age," special issue, *Journal of Negro Education* 86 (3): 252–68.

Logue, Josh. 2015. "Journalists as the Enemy." *Inside Higher Ed*, November 11. https://www.insidehighered.com/news/2015/11/11/video-shows-mizzou-student-press-clash-protesters.

Ludwig, Jens. 1998. "Political Booknotes." *Washington Monthly* 30 (6): 50–51.

Lukianoff, Greg, and Jonathan Haidt. 2015. "The Coddling of the American Mind." *Atlantic*, September. www.theatlantic.com/magazine/archive/2015/09/the-coddling-of-the-american-mind/399356.

Lunsford, Andrea. 2016. "Trigger Warnings, Safe Houses—and Writing." *Bedford Bits*, September 22. https://community.macmillan.com/community/the-english-community/bedford-bits/blog/2016/09/22/trigger-warnings-safe-houses-and-writing.

Ly, Laura. 2019. "Syracuse Students Are Camped Out in a Campus Building to Protest Racist Incidents." *CNN*, November 19. https://www.cnn.com/2019/11/19/us/syracuse-racist-incidents-protests-demands/index.html.

MacKinnon, Catharine. 2016. "In Their Hands: Restoring Institutional Liability for Sexual Harassment in Education." *Yale Law Journal* 125: 2038–105.

MacKinnon, Catharine, and Riva Siegel, eds. 2004. *Directions in Sexual Harassment Law.* New Haven, CT: Yale University Press.

Macrorie, Ken. 1974. *A Vulnerable Teacher.* Rochelle Park, NJ: Hayden Book Company.

Maraj, Louis M. 2020. *Black or Right: Anti/Racist Campus Rhetorics*. Louisville, CO: University Press of Colorado/Utah State University Press.

Marcotte, Amanda. 2013. "The Year of the Trigger Warning." *Slate*, December 30. www.slate.com/blogs/xx_factor/2013/12/30/trigger_warnings_from_the_feminist_blogosphere_to_shonda_rhimes_in_2013.html.

McElderry, Jonathan A., and Stephanie Hernandez Rivera. 2017. "'Your Agenda Item, Our Experience': Two Administrators' Insights on Campus Unrest at Mizzou." In "When Voices Rise: Race, Resistance, and Campus Uprisings in the Information Age," special issue, *Journal of Negro Education* 86 (3): 318–37.

McGee, Kate. 2021. "UT Hired Consultant for up to $1.1 Million to Revamp Battered Image of 'Eyes of Texas' Song." *KUT*, July 19. https://www.kut.org/education/2021-07-19/ut-hired-consultant-for-up-to-1-1-million-to-revamp-battered-image-of-eyes-of-texas-song.

McGill, Kevin. 2018. "Appeals Court Hears Challenge to Texas Campus Carry Law." *Lubbock Avalanche Journal*, July 11. https://www.lubbockonline.com/news/20180711/appeals-court-hears-challenge-to-texas-campus-carry-law.

McGough, Michael. 2015. "Opinion: No Safe Space for Reporters at University of Missouri Protest." *Los Angeles Times*, November 10. https://www.latimes.com/opinion/opinion-la/la-ol-missouri-protesters-reporters-20151110-story.html.

Meckler, Laura. 2018. "Betsy DeVos Set to Bolster Rights of Accused in Rewrite of Sexual Assault Rules." *Washington Post*, November 14. https://www.washingtonpost.com/local/education/betsy-devos-set-to-bolster-rights-of-accused-in-rewrite-of-sexual-assault-rules/2018/11/14/828ebd9c-e7d1-11e8-a939-9469f1166f9d_story.html.

Medina, Jennifer. 2014. "Warning: The Literary Canon Could Make Students Squirm." *New York Times*, May 17. www.nytimes.com/2014/05/18/us/warning-the-literary-canon-could-make-students-squirm.html.

Menand, Louis. 1996. *The Future of Academic Freedom*. Chicago: University of Chicago Press.

Merriam-Webster. 2017. s.v. "shock (*n.* 3)." http://www.merriam-webster.com/dictionary/shock.

Meyer, Heinz-Dieter. 2000. "Taste Formation in Pluralistic Societies: The Role of Rhetorics and Institutions." *International Sociology* 15 (1): 33–56.

Mi Gente. 2016. "Duke without Mi Gente." *Chronicle*, January 24. https://www.dukechronicle.com/article/2016/01/duke-without-mi-gente.

Milks, Megan. 2014. "On Trigger Warnings: A Roundtable." *Entropy Magazine*, April 14–18. http://web.archive.org/web/20220518072850/

https://entropymag.org/on-trigger-warnings-part-i-in-the-creative-writing-classroom/.

Mitra, Durba, and Catharine MacKinnon. 2018. "Ask a Feminist: Sexual Harassment in the Age of #MeToo." *Signs: Journal of Women in Culture and Society*, June 4. http://signsjournal.org/mackinnon-metoo.

Mone, Mark. 2016. "Chancellor's Update: UWM Stands Together." Office of the Chancellor, December 13. uwm.edu/chancellor/chancellors-update-uwm-stands-together.

Moody-Adams, Michele. 2015. "What's So Special about Academic Freedom?" In *Who's Afraid of Academic Freedom*, edited by Akeel Bilgrami and Jonathan Cole, 97–122. New York: Columbia University Press.

Muñoz, José Esteban. 2009. *Cruising Utopia: The Then and There of Queer Futurity*. New York: New York University Press.

National Center for Education Statistics. 2021a. "Race/Ethnicity of College Faculty." *Fast Facts*. https://nces.ed.gov/fastfacts/display.asp?id=61#.

National Center for Education Statistics. 2021b. "Table 329.10. On-Campus Crimes, Arrests, and Referrals for Disciplinary Action at Degree-Granting Postsecondary Institutions, by Location of Incident, Control and Level of Institution, and Type of Incident: Selected Years, 2001 through 2018." *Digest of Education Statistics*. https://nces.ed.gov/programs/digest/d20/tables/dt20_329.10.asp.

National Coalition Against Censorship. 2015. "What's All This about Trigger Warnings?" December. https://ncac.org/wp-content/uploads/2015/11/NCAC-TriggerWarningReport.pdf.

Ndemanu, Michael T. 2017. "Antecedents of College Campus Protests Nationwide: Exploring Black Student Activists' Demands." In "When Voices Rise: Race, Resistance, and Campus Uprisings in the Information Age," special issue, *Journal of Negro Education* 86 (3): 238–51.

Nealon, Jeffrey T. 2009. "The Economics of Academic Freedom, or Plato's P & T Committee." In "Academic Freedom," special issue, *South Atlantic Quarterly* 108 (4): 751–64.

Nelson, Scott, Chris Ortiz Y. Prentice, M. Catherine Coleman, Eric Detweiler, Marjorie Foley, Kendall Gerdes, Cleve Wiese, R. Scott Garbacz, and Matt King. 2013. "Crossing Battle Lines: Teaching Multimodal Literacies through Alternate Reality Games." *Kairos: A Journal of Rhetoric, Technology, and Pedagogy* 17, no. 3: http://technorhetoric.net/17.3/praxis/nelson-et-al/index.html.

Nish, Jennifer. 2022. *Activist Literacies: Transnational Feminisms and Social Media Rhetorics*. Columbia: University of South Carolina Press.

Northwestern Philosophy Graduate Student Association. 2017. "Letter to the Editor: Kipnis Book Misrepresents Grad Student, Employs Irresponsible Research." *Daily Northwestern*, April 23. https://daily

northwestern.com/2017/04/23/opinion/letter-to-the-editor-kipnis
-book-misrepresents-grad-student-employs-irresponsible-research/.

Norwood, Stephen H. 2011. *The Third Reich in the Ivory Tower: Complicity and Conflict on American Campuses.* New York: Cambridge University Press.

Nyong'o, Tav. 2015. "The Student Demand." *Bully Bloggers,* November 17. https://bullybloggers.wordpress.com/2015/11/17/the-student-demand/.

Oliviero, Katie. 2018. *Vulnerability Politics: The Uses and Abuses of Precarity in Political Debate.* New York: New York University Press.

Ore, Ersula. 2017. "Pushback: A Pedagogy of Care." *Pedagogy: Critical Approaches to Teaching Literature, Language, Composition, and Culture* 17 (1): 9–33.

Ore, Ersula. 2019. *Lynching: Violence, Rhetoric, and American Identity.* Jackson: University Press of Mississippi.

Orem, Sarah, and Neil Simpkins. 2015. "Weepy Rhetoric: Trigger Warnings and the Work of Making Mental Illness Visible in the Writing Classroom." *enculturation: a journal of rhetoric, writing, and culture* (20): https://enculturation.net/weepy-rhetoric.

Oxford English Dictionary. 2017. s.v. "shock (*v.* 2)." https://www.oed.com/view/Entry/178407.

Palfrey, John. 2017. *Safe Spaces, Brave Spaces: Diversity and Free Expression in Education.* Cambridge, MA: MIT Press.

Palus, Shannon. 2019. "The Latest Study on Trigger Warnings Finally Convinced Me They're Not Worth It." *Slate,* July 12. https://slate.com/technology/2019/07/trigger-warnings-research-shows-they-dont-work-might-hurt.html.

Patterson, Orlando. 1999. "When 'They' Are 'Us.'" *New York Times,* April 30. https://www.nytimes.com/1999/04/30/opinion/when-they-are-us.html.

Pearson, Michael. 2015. "A Timeline of the University of Missouri Protests." *CNN,* November 10. https://www.cnn.com/2015/11/09/us/missouri-protest-timeline/.

Pennie, Demetrick D. 2017. "Exploring College Leaders' Critical Incident Experiences Pursuant to Improving Campus Safety Policies during the Mass-Shooting Era." PhD diss., Texas Tech University.

Pérez-Peña, Richard, and Christine Hauser. 2015. "University of Missouri Professor Who Confronted Photographer Quits Journalism Post." *New York Times,* November 10. https://www.nytimes.com/2015/11/11/us/university-of-missouri-names-law-professor-to-diversity-post.html.

Peters, Jeremy W., Alexandra Alter, and Michael M. Gynbaum. 2017. "Milo Yiannopoulos's Pedophilia Comments Cost Him CPAC Role and Book Deal." *New York Times,* February 20. www.nytimes.com/2017/02/20/us/politics/cpac-milo-yiannopoulos.html.

Philipps, Dave. 2016. "What University of Texas Campus Is Saying about Concealed Guns." *New York Times,* August 28. https://www.nytimes .com/2016/08/28/us/university-of-texas-campus-concealed-guns.html.

Ponder, JoAnn. 2018. "From the Tower Shootings in 1966 to Campus Carry in 2016: Collective Trauma at the University of Texas at Austin." *International Journal of Applied Psychoanalytic Studies* 15 (4): 239–52.

Porter, James E., Patricia Sullivan, Stuart Blythe, Jeffrey T. Grabill, and Libby Milles. 2000. "Institutional Critique: A Rhetorical Methodology for Change." *College Composition and Communication* 51, no. 4 (June): 610–42.

Porter, Kamaria B., Sandra R. Levitsky, and Elizabeth A. Armstrong. 2023. "Gender Equity and Due Process in Campus Sexual Assault Adjudication Procedures." *Journal of Higher Education* 94 (2): 200–226.

Post, Robert C. 2012. *Democracy, Expertise, and Academic Freedom: First Amendment Jurisprudence for the Modern State.* New Haven, CT: Yale University Press.

Pratt, Mary Louise. 1991. "Arts of the Contact Zone." *Profession:* 33–40.

Prendergast, Catherine. 2009. "The Fighting Style: Reading the Unabomber's Strunk and White." *College English* 72 (1): 10–28.

Price, Margaret. 2001. *Mad at School: Rhetorics of Mental Disability and Academic Life.* Ann Arbor: University of Michigan Press.

Price, Margaret. 2021. "Time Harms: Disabled Faculty Navigating the Accommodations Loops." *South Atlantic Quarterly* 120, no. 1 (April): 257–77.

Pryal, Katie Rose Guest. 2010. "The Genre of the Mood Memoir and the *Ethos* of Psychiatric Disability." *Rhetoric Society Quarterly* 40 (5): 479–501.

Rainey, Homer P. 1971. *The Tower and the Dome: A Free University versus Political Control.* Boulder, CO: Pruett.

Rand, Erin. 2014. *Reclaiming Queer: Activist and Academic Rhetorics of Resistance.* Tuscaloosa: University of Alabama Press.

Randle, Aaron. 2019. "Racial Slurs, and the 15 Days That Shook Syracuse." *New York Times,* November 27. https://www.nytimes.com/2019/11/27/ nyregion/syracuse-university-racism.html.

Rankin, Kenrya. 2016. "STUDY: Student Activists Slowly Forcing University Presidents to Address Racial Disparities." *Colorlines,* March 17. https://www.colorlines.com/articles/study-student-activists-slowly -forcing-university-presidents-address-racial-disparities.

Read, Daphne. 1998. "Writing Trauma, History, Story: The Class(room) as Borderland." In "Exploring Borderlands: Postcolonial and Composition Studies," special issue, *JAC* 18 (1): 105–21.

Reichman, Henry. 2015. "On Student Academic Freedom." *Inside Higher*

Ed, December 4. www.insidehighered.com/views/2015/12/04/what -does-student-academic-freedom-entail-essay.

Reichman, Henry. 2019. *The Future of Academic Freedom*. Baltimore, MD: Johns Hopkins University Press.

Reynolds, Rema, and Darquillius Mayweather. 2017. "Recounting Racism, Resistance, and Repression: Examining the Experiences and #Hashtag Activism of College Students with Critical Race Theory and Counternarratives." In "When Voices Rise: Race, Resistance, and Campus Uprisings in the Information Age," special issue, *Journal of Negro Education* 86 (3): 283–304.

Ribeiro, Manoel Horta, Shagun Jhaver, Savvas Zannettou, Jeremy Blackburn, Emiliano De Cristofaro, Gianluca Stringhini, and Robert West. 2021. "Do Platform Migrations Compromise Content Moderation? Evidence from r/The_Donald and r/Incels." Paper presented at the Conference on Computer-Supported Cooperative Work and Social Computing, held virtually, October 23–27. https://arxiv.org/abs/2010.10397.

Richie, Beth E. 2000. "A Black Feminist Reflection on the Antiviolence Movement." In "Feminisms at a Millennium," special issue, *Signs* 25 (4): 1133–37.

Rojas, Fabio. 2007. *From Black Power to Black Studies: How a Radical Social Movement Became an Academic Discipline*. Baltimore, MD: Johns Hopkins University Press.

Rollins, Brooke. 2009. "Persuasion's Ethical Force: Levinas, Gorgias, and the Rhetorical Address." *JAC* 29, no. 3, 2009: 539–59.

Rollins, Brooke. 2020. *The Ethics of Persuasion: Derrida's Rhetorical Legacies*. Columbus: Ohio State University Press.

Ronell, Avital. 2002. *Stupidity*. Champaign: University of Illinois Press.

Rood, Craig. 2019. *After Gun Violence: Deliberation and Memory in an Age of Political Gridlock*. University Park: Pennsylvania State University Press.

Rood, Craig. 2020. "Addressing Gun Violence by Reimagining Masculinity and Protection." *Gender Policy Report*, September 22. https://gender policyreport.umn.edu/addressing-gun-violence-by-reimagining-mascu linity-and-protection/.

Rothfelder, Katy, and Davi Johnson Thornton. 2017. "Man Interrupted: Mental Illness Narrative as a Rhetoric of Proximity." *Rhetoric Society Quarterly* 47 (4): 359–82.

Royster, Jacqueline Jones. 1996. "When the First Voice You Hear Is Not Your Own." *CCC* 47 (1): 29–40.

Ruoppila, Sampo, and Albion M. Butters. 2021. "Not a 'Nonissue': Perceptions and the Realities of Campus Carry at the University of Texas at Austin." *Journal of American Studies* 55, no. 2 (May): 299–311.

Schlosser, Edward. 2015. "I'm a Liberal Professor, and My Liberal Students

Terrify Me." *Vox*, June 3. https://www.vox.com/2015/6/3/8706323/col
lege-professor-afraid.

Schmidt, Peter. 2015. "Colleges Respond to Racist Incidents as if Their
Chief Worry Is Bad PR, Studies Find." *Chronicle of Higher Education*,
April 21. https://www.chronicle.com/article/Colleges-Respond-to-Rac
ist/229517.

Schulman, Sarah. 2016. *Conflict Is Not Abuse: Overstating Harm, Community Responsibility, and the Duty of Repair.* Vancouver, BC: Arsenal Pulp.

Schwartz, Matthew S. 2020. "Trump Tells Agencies to End Trainings
on 'White Privilege' and 'Critical Race Theory.'" *NPR*, September 5.
https://www.npr.org/2020/09/05/910053496/trump-tells-agencies-to
-end-trainings-on-white-privilege-and-critical-race-theor.

Scott, Joan Wallach. 2019. *Knowledge, Power, and Academic Freedom.* New
York: Columbia University Press.

Sedgwick, Eve Kosofsky. 2003. *Touching Feeling: Affect, Pedagogy, and Performativity.* Durham, NC: Duke University Press.

Segalman, Bob, and Ralph Segalman. 1969. "The Riot That Did Not Happen—The Defused SDS National Conference (Austin, Texas)." Unpub-
lished paper, cited by permission from the authors. PDF file.

Sensoy, Özlem, and Robin DiAngelo. 2017. "'We Are All for Diversity,
but . . .': How Faculty Hiring Committees Reproduce Whiteness and
Practical Suggestions for How They Can Change." *Harvard Education
Review* 87 (4): 557–80.

Shapiro, Judith. 2014. "From Strength to Strength." *Inside Higher Ed*,
December 15. https://www.insidehighered.com/views/2014/12/15/
essay-importance-not-trying-protect-students-everything-may-upset
-them.

Sharp, Elizabeth, Shannon E. Weaver, and Anisa Zvonkovic. 2017. "Introduction to the Special Issue: Feminist Framings of Sexual Violence
on College Campuses." In "Feminist Framings of Sexual Violence on
College Campuses," special issue, *Family Relations* 66, no. 1 (February):
7–16.

Shields, Jon A., and Joshua M. Dunn Sr. 2016. *Passing on the Right: Conservative Professors in the Progressive University.* New York: Oxford University Press.

"Short Takes: Provocations on Public Feminism," on Laura Kipnis' *Unwanted Advances*, special feature of *Signs: Journal of Women in Culture and
Society*, July 2017. http://signsjournal.org/unwanted-advances/.

Shulevitz, Judith. "In College and Hiding From Scary Ideas." *New York
Times*, March 21. https://www.nytimes.com/2015/03/22/opinion/sun
day/judith-shulevitz-hiding-from-scary-ideas.html.

Sirc, Geoffrey. (1993) 2002. "Writing Classroom as A&P Parking Lot." *Pre-*

Text: A Journal of Rhetorical Theory 14: 27–70. Reprinted in *English Composition as a Happening*, 185–233. Logan: Utah State University Press.

Skinnell, Ryan. 2019. "Toward a Working Theory of Institutional Rhetorics." In *Reinventing (with) Theory in Rhetoric and Writing Studies: Essays in Honor of Sharon Crowley*, 69–82. Louisville, CO: University Press of Colorado/Utah State University Press.

Smith, Carly Parnitzke, and Jennifer J. Freyd. 2013. "Dangerous Safe Havens: Institutional Betrayal Exacerbates Sexual Trauma." *Journal of Traumatic Stress* 26: 113–24.

Solorzano, Daniel, Miguel Ceja, and Tara Yosso. 2000. "Critical Race Theory, Racial Microaggressions, and Campus Racial Climate: The Experiences of African American College Students." *Journal of Negro Education* 69, nos. 1/2: 60–73.

Somers, Patricia, and Nicholas Phelps. 2018. "Not Chilly Enough? Texas Campus Carry and Academic Freedom." *AAUP Journal of Academic Freedom* 9:1–15.

Stanley, Christine A. 2007. "When Counter Narratives Meet Master Narratives in the Journal Editorial-Review Process." *Educational Researcher* 36 (1): 14–24.

Stein, Kevin A., Matthew H. Barton, and Wm. Bryan Paul. 2017. "140 Characters to Say 'I Hate You': Melissa Click, Racism, and the Media Circus at Mizzou." *Relevant Rhetoric* 8: 1–16.

Steinem, Gloria. 1999. "Supremacy Crimes." *Ms.*, August/September.

"Support Resources for Faculty." 2013. *Oberlin College and Conservatory*, December 11. https://web.archive.org/web/20131222174936/http://new.oberlin.edu/office/equity-concerns/sexual-offense-resource-guide/prevention-support-education/support-resources-for-faculty.dot.

Syracuse University AAUP, Executive Council. 2019. "Letter to the Editor: SU Leadership Has Repeatedly Condemned Racism and Then Moved On." *Daily Orange*, November 17. http://w3w.dailyorange.com/2019/11/su-leadership-repeatedly-condemned-racism-moved/.

Táíwò, Olúfẹ́mi O. (@OlufemiOTaiwo). 2021. "anybody have a perspective on why we went with the term 'vulnerability'? am I the only one weirded out by why 'I should be able to wound you' ended up the guiding frame…" Twitter, November 27, 9:55 a.m., https://twitter.com/OlufemiOTaiwo/status/1464639063680503814.

Texas Association of School Boards Legal Services. 2022. "Firearms on School District Property." https://www.tasb.org/Services/Legal-Services/TASB-School-Law-eSource/Business/documents/firearms_on_dist_property.pdf.

Texas Standard. 2016. "Out of the Blue: 50 Years after the UT Tower Shooting." http://towerhistory.org/.

Thomason, Andy. 2015. "Amid Fears of Violence, Police in Missouri Arrest 2 Students over Threats on Yik Yak." *Chronicle of Higher Education*, November 11. https://www.chronicle.com/blogs/ticker/amid-fears-of-vio lence-u-of-missouri-police-arrest-man-over-threat-on-yik-yak/106570.

Thompson, Amy, James H. Price, Joseph A. Dake, Karen Teeple, Sara Bassler, Jagish Khubchandani, Dianne Kerr, et al. 2013. "Student Perceptions and Practices Regarding Carrying Concealed Handguns on University Campuses." *Journal of American College Health* 61 (5): 243–53.

Timmons, Patrick. 2016a. "Dildos on Campus, Gun in the Library: The *New York Times* and the Texas Gun War." *Counterpunch*, August 29. https://www.counterpunch.org/2016/08/29/dildos-on-campus-gun-in -the-library-the-new-york-times-and-the-texas-gun-war/.

Timmons, Patrick. 2016b. "Racism, Freedom of Expression and the Prohibition of Guns at Universities in Texas." *Counterpunch*, July 29. https:// www.counterpunch.org/2016/07/29/racism-freedom-of-expression-and -the-prohibition-of-guns-at-universities-in-texas/.

Title IX of the Education Amendments Act of 1972. Pub. L. No. 92-318, 86 Stat. 373 (1972) (codified as amended at 20 U.S.C. §§ 1681–1688 [2012]).

Tomlinson, Barbara. 2010. *Feminism and Affect at the Scene of Argument: Beyond the Trope of the Angry Feminist*. Philadelphia: Temple University Press.

US Department of Education Press Office. 2021. "Statement by US Department of Education Assistant Secretary for Civil Rights Catherine E. Lhamon on Title IX Update in Fall 2021 Unified Agenda and Regulatory Plan." December 10. https://www.ed.gov/news/press -releases/statement-us-department-education-assistant-secretary-office -civil-rights-catherine-lhamon-title-ix-update-fall-2021-unified-agenda -and-regulatory-plan.

Valentine, Matt. 2019. "The Growing Crisis of Guns on Campus." *New Republic*, March 22. https://newrepublic.com/article/153356/growing-cri sis-guns-campus.

Vitanza, Victor. 2011. *Sexual Violence in Western Thought and Culture: Chaste Rape*. New York: Palgrave Macmillan.

Vivian, Bradford. 2023. *Campus Misinformation: The Real Threat to Free Speech in American Higher Education*. New York: Oxford University Press.

Waller, Allyson. 2018. "Moving Forward: UT Professors Continue Legal Battle against Campus Carry Law." *Daily Texan*, April 20. https:// thedailytexan.com/2018/04/20/moving-forward-ut-professors-contin ue-legal-battle-against-campus-carry-law/.

Ward, LaWanda W. M., and Candace N. Hall. 2022. "Seeking Tenure while Black: Lawsuit Composite Counterstories of Black Professors at Historically White Institutions." *Journal of Higher Education* 93: 1012–36.

Warren, Calvin. 2018. *Ontological Terror: Blackness, Nihilism, and Emancipation.* Durham, NC: Duke University Press.

Weida, Jaime. 2018. "Free Speech, Safe Spaces, and Teaching in the Current US Political Climate." *AAUP Journal of Academic Freedom* 9: 1–13.

Weigel, Moira. 2016. "Political Correctness: How the Right Invented a Phantom Enemy." *Guardian,* November 30. https://www.theguardian .com/us-news/2016/nov/30/political-correctness-how-the-right-invent ed-phantom-enemy-donald-trump.

Weinstein, Adam. 2015. "The Secret History of the Campus Carry Movement." *Trace,* July 5. https://www.thetrace.org/2015/07/the-making-of -the-campus-carry-movement/.

Wendling, Mike. 2015. "Being 'Black on Campus'—Frustrations Spread across US." *BBC Trending.* November 12. https://www.bbc.com/news/ blogs-trending-34799061.

Williams, Cobretti. 2019. "Race and Policing in Higher Education." *Activist History Review,* November 19. https://activisthistory.com/2019/11/19/ race-and-policing-in-higher-education/.

Wilson, Robin. 2015. "Students' Requests for Trigger Warnings Grow More Varied." *Chronicle of Higher Education,* September 14. chronicle .com/article/Students-Requests-for/233043.

Womack, Anne-Marie. 2017. "Teaching Is Accommodation: Universally Designing Composition Classrooms and Syllabi." *CCC* 68 (3): 494–525.

Wu, Hong-An. 2016. "FemTechNet Statement in Support of Melissa Click and Concerned Student 1950." *FemTechNet,* June 1. http://femtechnet .org/2016/06/femtechnet-statement-in-support-of-melissa-click-and -concerned-student-1950/.

Yergeau, M. Remi. 2014. "Disable All the Things: On Affect, Metadata, and Audience." Keynote address presented at the Computers and Writing Conference, Washington State University, Pullman, WA. June 6.

Zahneis, Megan. 2018. "White-Supremacist Propaganda on Campuses Rose 77% Last Year." *Chronicle of Higher Education,* June 28. https:// www.chronicle.com/article/white-supremacist-propaganda-on-campus es-rose-77-last-year/.

Index

ability to respond, 14, 36
academic freedom, 16, 89, 90;
    accessibility, 29; appeals to,
    4, 7–9, 23, 26, 31, 41, 43, 49,
    50, 89; circulating in trig-
    ger warnings debate, 30–31;
    claims about, 16–17; failure in
    protecting intellectuals, 9; First
    Amendment right to, 74, 84;
    hospitality theory to, 32–33;
    Kipnis's article on, 49; as
    "marketplace of ideas," 17, 49;
    neoliberal view of, 4; relation-
    ship to rhetorical power, 9–10;
    relationship to sensitivity, 7, 8;
    student activism to, 60; threat
    to, 4, 17–18, 75, 83; in trigger
    warnings debate, 26; value of,
    22, 93. See also safe spaces;
    trigger warnings
*Activist Literacies: Transnational
    Feminisms and Social Media
    Rhetorics* (Nish), 11
affection: of language, 33, 34, 86; of
    others, 14, 53, 96n1; rhetorical,
    14–15, 19, 22, 33–36, 38–40,
    51, 86, 90, 91

Afro-Americans for Black Libera-
    tion, 77
agency, 7, 11, 33–34, 40, 43, 48, 69
Ahmed, Sara, 3, 5, 12, 21, 38–39,
    50, 89
Alexander, Jonathan, 13
Allen, Ira J., 14
alterity, 15, 39, 73, 91
American Association of Univer-
    sity Professors (AAUP), 25,
    60, 84
Anderson, Elizabeth, 44
anti-Black racism, 79–80
anti-immigrant racism, 79–80
Austin, J. L., 67
authority, 13, 24, 32, 45, 70; and
    whiteness, 56; instructors', 26,
    37, 39; rhetorical, 41; scientific,
    10
autonomy theory, 44

Bailie, Brian, 92
Balthaser, Benjamin, 95n4
Barnard, Ian, 97n5
Barnes, Aurora Temple, 84
Bates, Karen Grigsby, 61
Bedera, Nicole, 96n4